ENGAGED SPIRITUALITY

ENGAGED SPIRITUALITY

Faith Life in the Heart of the Empire

Joseph Nangle, O.F.M.

ORBIS BOOKS

Maryknoll, New York 10545

Second Printing, November 2008

Founded in 1970, Orbis Books endeavors to publish works that enlighten the mind, nourish the spirit, and challenge the conscience. The publishing arm of the Maryknoll Fathers and Brothers, Orbis seeks to explore the global dimensions of the Christian faith and mission, to invite dialogue with diverse cultures and religious traditions, and to serve the cause of reconciliation and peace. The books published reflect the views of their authors and do not represent the official position of the Maryknoll Society. To learn more about Maryknoll and Orbis Books, please visit our website at www.maryknoll.org.

Manufactured in the United States of America.
Manuscript editing and typesetting by Joan Weber Laflamme.

Library of Congress Cataloging-in-Publication Data

Nangle, Joseph.
        Engaged spirituality : faith life in the heart of the empire / Joseph Nangle.
              p. cm.
            13: 978-1-57075-763-1
          1. Spirituality—Catholic Church. 2. Spiritual life—Catholic Church.
3. Liberation theology. I. Title.
            BX2350.65.N36 2008
            248.4'82—dc22

                                                                    2007040378

To Gustavo Gutiérrez, O.P.,
priest, theologian, and prophet,
who opened for me the social implications
of Jesus' life and message
&
To my dearest friend,
Marie Dennis,
for sharing the inward and outward journey
over more than three decades.

Contents

viii   *Contents*

Acknowledgments

● ● ● ● ● ● ● ● ● ●

The long story of this book began and continues with the many women and men, lay and religious, who have engaged with me in spiritual retreats. To each of them my lasting gratitude for his or her patience and valuable responses to what I had to say. I thank, too, the friend who urged me to write about the inner journey, which has run parallel to my active life in Latin America and the United States. My gratitude to Robert Ellsberg, editor and publisher of Orbis Books, who never settles for mediocrity. My appreciation to Beverly Choltco-Devlin, Siobhan Dugan, and Brighid O'Brien, who helped me greatly with researching the references for the notes. Finally, thanks to Joan Laflamme, whose copy editing skills proved enormously helpful in the final version of the book.

A Bit of History

Three years ago, when I finished writing *Birth of a Church*, the account of my eleven years as founding pastor of Most Holy Name Parish in Lima, Peru, a friend asked an interesting question: "You've written about your outward journey; shouldn't you share something of the inner journey that you surely walked during those eventful years?"

My immediate reaction was to reject the idea. I felt that our culture has quite enough "me-centered" treatises. Who needs one more, I asked myself.

However, as I thought more about the question, my friend's point intrigued me and made me take a second look. I knew, for example, that a very important follow-up to the intense experiences I had during those years in Lima was the opportunity to share them in the context of retreats, days of recollection, homilies, and conferences beginning almost immediately upon my return to the United States. In particular, the leader of a women's religious congregation in this country visited Most Holy Name Parish in Lima just as I was finishing my time there and practically insisted that I conduct a retreat for her sisters back home. That experience, which seemed to go well, began a thrust in my life and ministry that continues to the present. Indeed, for a few years, retreat work, particularly with diocesan and religious priests, was my principal activity. Most other times it has remained one of a variety of ministries I have done. In addition, I have found myself getting called on regularly to give conferences and days of recollection on what I began to call engaged spirituality.

Preaching retreats and offering days of recollection or conferences on spirituality mean, of course, serious reflection on what one has to say—on the inner journey one has walked and on the convictions which one has come to. In my case that journey had everything to do with the life-changing events of my four years in Bolivia and eleven in Peru. I went to South America as one sort of Franciscan priest and returned very much another—a common experience in the life of all missioners who let the world and the people they encounter in the host country and culture affect them deeply.

In addition, my providential encounter with the methodology of liberation theology during the years I spent in Peru—using one's own experience and that of others to challenge, question, demand answers (or as the rich Spanish word expresses it *interpelar*), of God's word and religious doctrines—gave me a way to proceed, a way of organizing such an important event as a retreat. Thinking through and outlining the various topics of a retreat, I regularly reached into my memory bank for the insights and convictions and ways of presenting the various aspects of spirituality that I had come to in Latin America, and I spoke from that font. This preaching ministry became for me another example of the wonderful phrase from St. Bernard of Clairvaux (which theologian Gustavo Gutiérrez used as the title of his own book on spirituality): "we drink from our own wells." Time and again I went back to the well I had gradually dug during fifteen years in Latin America, and I accessed my own inner journey to figure out what I might have to offer.

Sometimes this approach produced surprise in my audiences. I remember in particular one bishop who made a retreat that I preached in a certain U.S. archdiocese. He was a very meticulous person and took extensive notes during each of my conferences. At the final session on the last day the schedule called for the retreatants to share their reactions to what they had heard in my twice-daily conferences. When the bishop's turn came, he sort of shook his head over the pages he had written and said, "I'm not sure what to do with all of this." Thoughts about spirituality that come out of one's experiences, out of one's own well, don't always square with neat, preconceived, mental slots.

So, despite some initial misgivings, I began to think that perhaps my friend's suggestion—writing about the inner journey that ran alongside the outer one I shared in *Birth of a Church*—had merit. In the years following my return from Latin America, as I gained distance from and perspective on them, I had become increasingly aware of the profound conversion that took place in me during the remarkable decade and one half I spent there. I thought that people might find that story useful for their own journeys. Moreover, thanks to those numerous retreats and similar activities with various lay, religious, and priests' groups in the United States, I felt that I could speak about that inner journey with some precision, and, I hoped, clarity.

U.S. American Spirituality Today

Furthermore, in thinking about all of this, I felt that I might make a contribution to the vast amount of work that is continually going on in the field of spirituality. My reading, admittedly limited, of the literature on this subject had convinced me that in our so-called developed world, particularly in the United States, spiritual writers and practitioners tend to concentrate on the individual. An amazing amount of attention goes to concerns regarding one's own life in God, one's development as a person, the obstacles in the way of realizing one's full potential. We put great emphasis on an individualistic, highly psychologized—not to say narcissistic—approach to spiritual matters. In this culture, I came to believe, spirituality seems to be basically "all about me."

Around that time I came across a catalogue from a Catholic renewal center in the United States. The list of upcoming events included solidly spiritual opportunities like Bible study, contemplative prayer, as well as directed, preached, and private retreats—all calibrated to individual tastes and wishes. At the same time the schedule for one three-month period included a whole lot that I thought was exceedingly me-centered: spiritual solutions to weight loss, t'ai chi, health and harmony, healing anxiety and isolation, mind over mood, and so on, and so on. Admittedly, a spiritual renewal center by definition deals with the many facets of achieving individual spiritual, emotional, and physical well-being and integration. But I really didn't see in the listings much balance between this concentration on the individual and concern for the neighbor, the other, much less for the larger, hurting world that surrounds us. In checking similar brochures I found that this menu varies little from typical offerings in our first-world retreat houses and spirituality centers.

My inner journey, on the other hand, had taken me in a quite different direction. Within the framework of a reality (Latin America) that was dependent, oppressed, and impoverished, and with the tools for reflection provided by social analysis, liberation theology, and conscientization, as well as the day-to-day pastoral work in which I had engaged there, spirituality had come to mean for me a life in God that was necessarily "other oriented"; its center of gravity had to be outside of oneself. A stanza of St. Francis's "Peace Prayer" best emphasized the difference for me: "O Divine Master, let me not so much seek to be consoled as to console, to be understood as to understand, to be loved as to love." Sharing this quite different experience of mine, I thought, might be a contribution—not to say antidote—to a lot of what is written and discussed today under the rubric of spirituality, especially in our so-called developed world.

So I decided to take a crack at writing something between a personal journal and a text on spirituality as I had come to understand it. This first-person account will be one of two threads—two story lines—woven through the pages of this book. I do hope it does not come across as "all about me." My intention is quite the contrary. I believe that spirituality in the end is mostly about the other—the Other who is God and the other who is sister and brother, especially when he or she is hurting and in need. As someone once said, Christians should conjugate the verb *to be* differently: *you* should always come before *I*, biologically, emotionally, intellectually, and yes, spiritually. And when that *you* is part of the incalculable number of oppressed, marginalized, diminished, hurting human beings in our world, then that *you* definitely comes before me.

What I have tried to do in this modest volume is to offer my perspective on the traditional categories of Catholic-Christian spirituality—prayer, Eucharist, spiritual reading, and so on—in the context of our contemporary world. This approach flows directly from a description of spirituality that I heard and identified with many years ago in South America: "Spirituality means life in the Holy Spirit who, far from being ignorant of or absent from or indifferent to current reality, has a loving concern for the here and now, messy, disorganized state of our world." In this view spirituality has to be "engaged" with reality or it is not life in the Spirit.

Spirituality Lived in the Empire

Furthermore, and ever so much more important, this "other-oriented" life in God struck me as crucial for Catholic-Christians in the industrialized world, particularly for those of us who live in the United States. We live in the world's only superpower, a country that the rest of the world increasingly describes as an empire, in the same way former world powers like England, Spain, and of course Rome held that title. No less a theologian than Jesuit Jon Sobrino describes the phenomenon this way: "Today's empire is the United States. It imposes its will on the whole planet, with immense power. Its mystique is its triumph over all others."[1] This empire, like the ones that came before it, has its legions—transnational corporations, multinational lending agencies, and other countries that in the words of President Bush, are "coalitions of the willing." But the United States stands at the center of all these and drives them with economic, military, and political power.

Robert Kagan, a senior associate at the Carnegie Foundation for International Peace, has just written a hefty book entitled *Dangerous Nation* on the subject of America as empire. In a *Washington Post* review, history professor David M. Kennedy summarizes Kagan's thesis: "As the nation grew more powerful, its dreams became desires; desires became necessities; necessities became imperatives; and imperatives led to empire—in the fullest sense of the word. . . . And when a nation arrives at the point in its history when it believes itself to possess unmatchable power and harbors no doubts about the scope of its interests or the rightness of its cause . . . what dangers does it court for itself, as well as for others?"[2]

I know that many in our society reject the idea of the United States as empire. We don't like to think of ourselves that way. Our self-image is altogether benign. However, as people of faith living in this country, anything less than a spirituality that acknowledges and deals with our status as empire I believe has to be found wanting. We simply cannot continue to withdraw into some sort of privatized, head-in-the-sand understanding of what it means to believe in the God of Jesus, who came to call nations to the peace of God's reign. Because of our place and time in history a most challenging burden has fallen on us who are church: continually to speak and live a prophetic word in the very heart of this latest empire, the United States. We certainly did not choose this role and perhaps would prefer not to play it. But it is unavoidably ours, it is urgent, and we shall be judged on how faithful we were to it.

So, a second thread or story line—the pressing need for a prophetic word from people who try to live our faith in this place and this time—will run through the pages of this book as well. I believe that the greatest sin committed by people of faith in the U.S. empire today is the omission of that challenging word. By and large our bishops, priests, religious women and men, and many lay people lack the training and the inclination to critique this empire, one which has the capacity for much good in the world but which in fact is doing so much harm. The training and willingness to take on such a prophetic challenge and duty come in the first place from a spirituality that engages with reality— in this case, our reality, which Pope John Paul II described as "a culture of death."

I want to insist, however, that this book is not just an exercise in social analysis or social commentary. Those sorts of reflections have a rightful place here. But this book is about nothing more or less than spirituality—life in God, who, we believe, is vitally interested and engaged in our here-and-now, real-life business. It is based on the Christian understanding of God who "so loved the world that he gave his only Son . . . not to condemn the world, but in order that the world might be saved through him" (Jn 3:16–17).

A final thought. A couple of years ago a young theologian on the faculty of Georgetown University, Vincent Miller, wrote a challenging book entitled *Consuming Religion: Christian Faith and Practice in a Consumer Culture.*[3] In it, Miller continually uses the word *commodification* to describe the growing tendency in our culture to see everything, including religion and spirituality, as a commodity: consumer items, a constant exercise in picking and choosing, a series of buyers' preferences.

If I had one fervent hope for this book, it would be that it not be read with a consumerist's mentality, as just one more commodity on the religious supermarket shelf marked spirituality. What I offer here on the authority, for better or worse, of my own lived experience and that of so many others who have come into direct contact with our hurting world is a view of spirituality made up of whole cloth. I know that is a long reach, even one that smacks of arrogance. However, I have seen and believe firmly that an other-oriented spirituality in a world where too often the other is oppressed, needy, marginalized or threatened, is not only possible but stands at the very heart of what Jesus meant when he said: "No one has greater love than this, to lay down one's life for one's friends" (Jn 15:13). Moreover, an other-oriented spirituality, I believe, offers the best hope for the people of this self-seeking, domineering, terribly fearful empire to redeem our very souls.

Chapter 1

• • • • •

The Incarnation

A Question

During the years that I worked in Lima, we had the good for-
tune to have a dedicated and skilled sister-nurse from the United
States come to join our parish team and begin to work among the
large number of sick poor people in the area. At a team meeting
a few weeks into her ministry the sister spoke up and told the
rest of us about some serious doubts she had begun to have.

"When I look at that endless line of sick people who show up
at the parish clinic each day," she said, "I know that even if I
could take care of all their health problems—which I can't—the
line will never get any shorter. I know we are immersed in the
world of the poorest here. But, what is worse," she continued, "is
when I look at life through the eyes of all those impoverished and
sick people, I see no evidence whatsoever of the loving God who
is supposed to care for human beings more than the lilies of the
fields and the birds of the air. Where is that God for them?"

The rest of us on the parish team understood immediately
what the sister was saying. It was as if she was putting into
words much of what we had thought but hadn't yet articulated
in our own daily contacts with the sea of poverty all around us.
Each of us knew hundreds of people who lived subhuman lives.
They came to the parish office every day looking for help—a job,
medicine, a ride to the hospital, money for food, clothing. In that
city and country of the two-thirds world the glaring poverty of
the majority living there was in our faces every hour of every day.

Their needs were endless. So that evening and for a long time afterward each one of us on the parish team wrestled with the sister's burning question, her crisis of faith: where is this Mother/Father God in the lives of all these suffering people?

It is clear that the same question eventually gets asked by anyone who takes life seriously and that it is not at all confined to certain parts of the world. We heard the question after the devastating tsunami of December 2004 and when Hurricane Katrina wiped out vast areas of the southern United States. How many times we have heard it and asked it when a healthy infant dies suddenly, or a child gets terminal cancer, or a heart attack takes the life of a young father, or a woman comes down with debilitating, chronic disease, or a beloved elderly person lingers through an apparently meaningless dying process. We ask, why do these things happen? Where is God in all of this?

And aren't the same hard questions asked about the larger and broader pain in the world? Don't we wonder where God is when we hear of the near starvation that millions suffer in places like Darfur and Niger; or the racism that continues to marginalize people of color in Europe and the United States; or the sexism and enslavement of women and children that begin in places like Thailand and spill across to the industrialized West; or the overdevelopment and underdevelopment side by side in cities like Washington DC and Buenos Aires all across the globe; or the pollution of the air, water, and soil on our planet; or wars, genocide, abuse of children, terrorism, abortion, torture? The list goes on and on, and so does the questioning about where is God.

We ask the questions, and the questions challenge us to the core of our beings, to the core of our faith life. They challenge us particularly when we in the United States realize that in many instances our way of life produces the very problems we are asking about. We live in the most affluent society human history has ever known at the very same time that literally billions of women and men around the world languish in hunger, poverty, and despair. In that light the questions about why these conditions continue, where God is in all of this, and how God can allow things like this, confront us U.S. Americans directly. As a member of my own order in the Third World put it one time: "How can you be a Franciscan and live in New York?" He couldn't put together life in the United States with following St. Francis of Assisi.

Religious traditions with their accompanying spiritualities are supposed to provide some answers, shed some light, offer some insights on where God is. Otherwise those traditions and their spiritualities will be found inadequate, fatally flawed, and useless. The many attempts today to craft a "be happy, don't worry" me-centered spirituality totally ignore these deeper concerns and demands on faith. What happens, then, is that when people come face to face with life's hardest and ultimate challenges, like those mentioned above, they find themselves forced to seek answers elsewhere—in escapism, or in some brand of other-worldly or New Age mysticism. More practical people often just drop the whole business of spirituality and immerse themselves in advocating social change for its own sake. Others throw in the towel and live disengaged and unexamined lives. Faith and spirituality have failed them all.

The Christian "Answer"—The Cornerstone of Spirituality

When we in Lima long ago came up against the really awful dilemma of wondering, indeed doubting, about Jesus' loving Abba-Father in the lives and experience of the sick and poor in the so-called Third World, we reached for and with the help of God found something that helped us. It was not a pat answer, but it was a ray of light, some inspiration, a way of coping with what could have been the paralyzing consequences of doubts about whether God was really there for the dreadfully poor of our neighborhood, our city, and the world. We rediscovered the incarnation. But it wasn't the disembodied theological formulation "God-became-man" that we had learned by rote in our catechisms or that we had recited mechanically in the creed. It was a new discovery of a living, breathing, loving, passionate, and compassionate God who joined with humanity and shared all of our brokenness. That incredible truth became a lifeline as our daily encounters with the poorest of the poor inevitably continued.

For me, this rediscovery marked a return to something that had long before made a significant impact on my faith life. Early in my Franciscan journey I had come to a body-soul conviction that the incarnation of God in Jesus was true—absolutely true. From that moment on it was not simply something others had told me or, much less, a bloodless article of faith. God-with-us became a driving force in my life. I never afterward lost that conviction. Indeed, it deeply influenced everything: how I looked at the world, my vows as a Franciscan, my choice to become a priest, volunteering for work in South America. But now, surrounded by third-world sick and poor people, the incarnation took on a wider and far deeper significance. Seeing "emmanuel" in light of the world of pain in which I had become immersed brought an almost indescribable new awareness of just who—and where—this God is. He/She is right here with us, especially with the poor.

Little by little I came to see, also, that grasping afresh the consequences of a God who becomes one of us holds out a lifeline for those of us who live in this world of privilege and comfort and, yes, imperialism. We may not like what this core Christian belief demands of us, but it is our only real hope, as I'll try to show in the rest of this chapter.

Thanks to that defining experience in my life, I'm convinced that both in the world of impoverishment and in the world of overabundance the best place to start to lay out a spirituality that is vitally engaged with the world is this cornerstone of Christian faith, the incredible affirmation that God has become one with us. Not to probe this claim, I believe, is to miss the whole point of salvation history. Not to probe it leaves us helplessly paralyzed and even cynical in the face of the enormity of human pain. Not to probe it is to condemn ourselves to depressing worries about the value of anything but a selfish and self-centered life, worries that preoccupy so many people in the affluent world. At the end of the day, at the end of our lives, I believe the question for each of us will be: did my life have meaning? And the danger, particularly in our pleasure-seeking First World, lies in the possibility that we will have to answer that question in the negative.

Put positively, to look at the incarnation and really think about its relevance for all of the disturbing, unsettling, and doubt-producing dilemmas of our existence is to lay the foundation for a spirituality that I believe, can drive us and sustain us in personal and societal struggles for "life more abundantly" (Jn 10:10) on behalf of the poorest, the neglected, and yes, in the end on behalf of our own selves. The consequences of God's coming among us give meaning to our lives, even and especially in the heart of the empire. In the light, then, of this true story about the sick poor in Lima, Peru, and of numberless similar stories from each of our life's experiences, we take a look once again at this incredible claim our tradition makes: God is truly, personally among us.

A Completely Incarnate God

We Catholic-Christians say that we live by the belief in God who became human in the person of Jesus the Christ; we hold that the Creator became part of creation; we claim that the divine Word has become flesh "and made his dwelling among us" (Jn 1:14). We say that the transcendent Other, the One Who Is (Ex 3:14), that God, the Source of all being, eternal Word, and sanctifying Spirit, all-present, almighty, all-knowing, totally beyond our comprehension, became a person like us in Jesus of Nazareth. This startling affirmation has enormous consequences that, as we've already seen, go to the heart of our questions about God's interest in and presence with the poor, the miserable, the neglected of our societies—and to the heart of our questions about God's concern for each of us. The claim of God-with-us questions our world and our lives that in many ways live off the backs of the poor.

When we think concretely about what this belief in an incarnate God means, the mind bends. It's such a bold belief for humans. Because God's incarnation is just that—an enfleshing of the Divine just the way all of humanity is enfleshed, through the natural process of conception, gestation, and birth. We hold that God in the person of Jesus was an embryo, a fetus, a newborn, an infant. He became a growing boy, an adult in formation; a relational human being; a friend, and yes, an enemy. He died a horrible death and was buried in someone else's grave. He knew what to be human is. The concrete reality of the incarnation is so amazing and far-reaching that it challenges our credence.

About twenty years ago I met a middle-aged priest who years before had converted to Catholicism from the Episcopalian tradition. I was interested to hear his story, especially his reasons for coming over to the Roman church from one that so closely resembles it in its teachings and liturgical practices. He told me that as a young man he had served for a few years as an Episcopalian priest, but that in his thirties he ran into a vocational crisis. Taking a leave of absence from the ministry, he went on an extended vacation/pilgrimage to Europe. One day, he told me, in the crypt of a cathedral in Rheims he came upon a life-sized statue of a young and very pregnant woman. When he asked a bystander whom she represented, the answer came back, "Why of course that's Mary, the mother of Jesus."

The priest said that his immediate reaction was annoyance. "Those d—n Roman Catholics," he thought, "they *would* get in your face with that kind of graphic depiction of Mary's pregnancy, wouldn't they?" But, he said, as he thought more about the statue, he began to realize that for nine months in human history the only clue to God's becoming human was a young, pregnant, Jewish woman. That realization became his gateway to Catholicism and to a lifetime of great enthusiasm for the role of Mary in bringing God into the world of humans. I happened to have this conversation with him on the eve of a particular feast day of Mary, and he was obviously very animated in preparing to celebrate it. The man had come to understand the normal, flesh and blood—can we even say the down and dirty?—aspects of incarnation.

The conjoining of God with humanity also means that our Creator has undergone everything that human experience contains—all of our joys and sorrows, our hopes and failures, our agonies and triumphs, our dreams and frustrations. For example, in Jesus, God was a growing child. The story about his three-day absence as a twelve year old from Mary and Joseph's company and his mother's very typical question when she found her son— "Why have you done this to us?" (Lk 2:48)—speak volumes about the normal fits and starts all of us go through in developing into adult human beings. Jesus lived every bit of the growing-up process.

He had to discover his vocation in life as well. I once heard a student of scripture talk about the scene at the Jordan River when John the Baptist pointed to Jesus as the "Lamb of God" (Jn 1:29). The scholar made a big point about the stunning revelation that was for the carpenter from Nazareth. As an observant Jew, Jesus knew that John was making a direct reference to the prophet Isaiah in his regard: "Like a lamb led to the slaughter or a sheep before the shearers, he was silent and opened not his mouth" (Is 53:7). John was prophesying that he, Jesus, would be the one to take on the sins of his people as the Suffering Servant, and that new information drove him at once out into the desert for an extended period of prayer and fasting. It's no wonder that during the forty days of that desert experience Jesus experienced searing temptations based on physical hunger, lust for power, and cravings for prestige (cf. Lk 4) to turn away from such a fearful vocation. They were real inducements, just like the ones we have, to unfaithfulness.

Emmanuel—God-with-us—comes across as healthily relational, too. He loved life; he liked people; people liked him. The Gospels are filled with evidence of this. When Jesus selects a tax collector, Levi, as one of his twelve special collaborators, the man throws a great party in his home, at which Jesus seems entirely, scandalously for some, comfortable among all of the unsavory characters that show up (Mt 9:9ff.). In a different context it's revealing to note Jesus' very human response when he comes upon the heart-rending scene of a widow in the town of Naim as she walks alongside the body of her only son as he's being carried to his grave. Before Jesus acts to bring the boy back from the dead, the Gospel tells us, "he was moved with pity and said to her 'do not cry.'" Then, after raising the young man, "Jesus gave him back to his mother" (Lk 7:11–15). The Gospels are full of touching little details like these that point to a highly sensitive, relational man.

The case of the woman caught in an adulterous act (Jn 8:1–11) also demonstrates the humanness of Jesus. Not only did he confront the hypocrisy of her accusers, including, no doubt, the man who had been found with her ("let the man among you who has no sin be the first to cast a stone at her"), but he treated her with sincerity and respect as well: "Has no one condemned you? . . . Nor do I condemn you." We can only imagine the relief and gratitude that surged in that poor woman's heart when she heard those words from the Teacher. Or imagine the sentiments of another woman when she heard Jesus defend her in front of the hypocritical and judgmental men sitting at table in Simon the Pharisee's home, "Her many sins are forgiven because of her great love," and as he turned and said to her, "Your faith has been your salvation. Now go in peace" (Lk 7:36–50). It's not hard to see the influence of Jesus' own mother and how much she did to make her son a considerate and sensitive human being when we read these real-life events in the Gospels.

This son of a carpenter, Joseph, and a carpenter himself, attracted working men like him. The fisher folks around Capernaum must already have taken notice of him as he moved along the shores of the lake where they made their livelihood. When he called to them, "Come after me" (Mk 1:17), they immediately threw down their nets and went with him. Grown men don't usually take such a leap into something new, so their attitude speaks volumes about the charism and qualities of leadership they must have seen in Jesus. The Lord also felt a kinship with the young man who said that he had observed the commandments since childhood. Jesus "loved him" and invited the youth to an even deeper relationship with him: "Sell what you have, give it to the poor . . . then come follow me" (Mk 10:21).

Jesus knew special friendships too. He certainly had the unique experience of intimacy that comes along from time to time in life. He loved Martha and Mary and their brother Lazarus, stayed at their home when he could, and wept with the sisters as they mourned Lazarus's death—a reaction that made the bystanders remark, "See how much he loved him" (Jn 11:36). Even among his closest collaborators he had his favorites—Peter, Andrew, James, and especially John, the "beloved disciple."

He had his dislikes, as well. As Judas gradually demonstrated his flawed character, helping himself to the group's money, Jesus warned him: "one of you is a devil" (Jn 6:70). And as he shared a Last Supper with his friends, Jesus knew which one of the twelve would shortly turn him in to the authorities, "The hand of my betrayer is with me at this table" (Lk 22:21). He even told

Judas, "Be quick about what you are to do"(Jn 13:27). A failed relationship, beyond retrieval; a betrayal by someone whom he had invited into his inner circle—he experienced it all.

From the moment that I saw, really saw, this reality of the human-divine person who was Jesus of Nazareth, life's basic task became totally clear to me. I knew that in light of God becoming human, we're all supposed to be as fully human as possible— that's our purpose. I had read spiritual writers who put this call in terms such as "the imitation of Christ" or "following in the footsteps of Jesus." All well and good, but basically I came to believe that the task for each of us is to embrace our humanness and love it, because God embraced it and loved it. Then we have to allow, help, and inspire others to do the same. In the end, this is what Jesus was and did. He was a complete human person, fully alive, and his mission was to help all those around him to be the same. The thrilling line from John's Gospel says it so well: "I came that they may have life, and have it to the full" (Jn 10:10).

Now, with this deeper insight into the incarnation that came as the result of a sister's question that evening in Peru, the awful plight of the poor in our world and the conditions of subhumanity that produced their plight stood as an insult to what Jesus was about, a blasphemy against God who "so loved the world that he gave his only Son" (Jn 3:16). If Jesus came so that every person could live and develop and become whom God intended her or him to be, then all of the poverty, violations, and oppressions suffered by those who never get a chance at life make a mockery of God-with-us. This growing conviction stirred in all of us, a real outrage at the injustice of all the half-lives we were seeing around us.

On several occasions since returning from Peru I've heard criticisms of missioners who come back to the United States with that rage very close to the surface. But if ever there was reason for anger, the plight of poor women, children, and men condemned to subhuman lives was it. We had seen firsthand the results of oppression among people whose names we knew. We also know that the lifestyle and policies and economics of the so-called developed world contribute in no small way to those oppressions. What kind of a human being and believer in the Incarnate

One could not feel indignation at such impoverishment and the reasons for it?

Politically Incarnate as Well

To pick up on that last insight—the reasons for human degradation—what we don't hear enough in reflections on this totally human God, the Word become flesh, is that he knew and responded to the social, political, and economic circumstances of his times as well. It's amazing that we don't hear about it, because this facet of his life stands as the most dramatic and certainly the most consequential of all. He was a Jew of first-century Palestine, a citizen of an occupied country under the twin domination of Roman imperialists and their local religious collaborators, the chief priests, scribes, Pharisees, and doctors of the Law. The story of Jesus' three years of public ministry is primarily one of his increasing anger and conflict with the power structure of his country—precisely because that structure was so demeaning for most of the people.

From the beginning of that ministry there were serious disputes between Jesus and the established order. For example, early on he returned to his hometown of Nazareth after a short sojourn around the Galilean countryside and proclaimed that Isaiah's prophecy of "a day of the Lord's favor" was being fulfilled in him, right there in their midst. He was saying that the time of the final Jubilee had come, when all of the injustices and imbalances and inequities that had piled up would be redressed. It seems that the townsfolk understood that Jesus was ready to upset the status quo—which he was—so they rushed him to the top of the cliff above Nazareth and tried to throw him off (Lk 4:29–30). Beginning there at the threshold of Jesus' public life all of the Gospels give example after example of Jesus' criticisms of his country's social, economic, and religious structures during the three years of his preaching. As that preaching and his actions became more and more publicized and the powerful rightly saw him as a threat to the established order, his life was increasingly in danger until finally "his hour had come" and he allowed them to capture, torture, and kill him.

In human terms that tragic ending to Jesus' ministry and life did not happen because he was preaching a message of love—though he certainly was doing that. It happened because he was applying the message of love to the concrete, socio-political realities of his time and place. His love for the poor made Jesus take their side, speak for them, draw attention to them. Standing outside the Temple one day, he pointed out to his disciples the situation of a poor woman contributing two copper coins "from her want" and celebrating her instead of celebrating the rich, who were making "contributions from their surplus" to God's house (Lk 21:1–4).

He loved those who wielded power in his world, too, but that love had a realistic and stern edge to it (today we would call it tough love): "Woe to you scribes and Pharisees, you frauds . . . blind fools . . . blind guides . . . vipers' nest . . . brood of serpents" (Mt 23). And the ones who had most to lose, the members of the socio-political establishment of the time, reacted to Jesus' challenge with increasing hostility until finally they came to a critical analysis and judgment: "If we let him go on like this, the whole world will believe in him. Then the Romans will come in and sweep away our sanctuary and our nation. . . . It is better . . . to have one man die [for the people] than to have the whole nation destroyed." And then the Gospel goes on to say, "From that day onward there was a plan afoot to kill him" (Jn 11:48–53). This practical, calculated, political decision came just before Jesus' arrest and sentencing.

So for anyone who believes that God has become an integral part of our existence some very real and enormously challenging conclusions follow. We're not people who worship some remote divine Being, someone who is absent from, or ignorant of, or indifferent to humanity's processes, hopes, struggles, successes, and disasters. We hold that in seeing Jesus and his total identification with our personal, interpersonal, and socio-historical realities, we see God present and vitally interested in those realities.

The incarnation remains a mystery, a matter of faith. This belief in God's immanence, God's "here and nowness" was not a completely satisfying answer to the sister-nurse's doubts—and our doubts—about a provident God in the lives of third-world

poor. Nor is it a total answer to the searing questions that face
us as citizens of the U.S. empire. The mystery of sin and evil and
tragedy in human lives remains very much with us. But to have
found a living faith in the proposition that God walked life's journey and experienced everything that is human gave us enough to
hang on to back then in Lima. We took up anew and with immense purpose our solidarity with and concern for those numberless poor people who surrounded us daily.

I believe that this cornerstone of Christian faith can point the
way in our First World as well. If God has become one of us, then
all human beings enjoy almost divine dignity. And we who pros-
per on this earth need to pay attention to the ones who do not
—otherwise, God is mocked. I believe the incarnation helps all
of us here and now to face the fact that our world is upside down
and needs to be righted. I'm convinced, therefore, that a living,
practical faith in God's incarnation serves as the indispensable
grounding for an engaged, outward-oriented spirituality lived in
the heart of the empire.

Dimensions of Life— Personal, Interpersonal, Social

It's important to probe a little further some of the practical
consequences that came into focus for me as a result of a renewed belief that God became one of us in Jesus the Christ.
Three dimensions of human experience come to mind when we
think about the incarnation and our lives. The first two of these
are so self-evident as not to need detailing. But for the sake of
lifting up in a particular way the third dimension of life, let me
mention the first two briefly.

On the most obvious level of experience there is the personal.
Jesus and we have our own particular, individual responses to the
events of our lives. Just as Luke's Gospel says of Jesus, all of us
have to progress in "wisdom and age and grace" (Lk 2:52) as we
mature. We have to figure out our place in the world and what
God asks of us—just as Jesus did. Each of us inherits and devel-
ops a particular personality—like Mary's Son did. There is no
mystery in this natural process of moving from birth through

childhood, adolescence, and on to adulthood; what is remarkable is that God in Jesus experienced it as well. As this chapter emphasizes, his was a completely human and unique personality—the same as each of ours. That's what I mean by the personal dimension of life.

A second dimension of the human experience that comes naturally to mind in reflecting on God's incarnation as a man and our own journeys through life is the interpersonal. A complex network of family, neighbors, friends, teachers, mentors, acquaintances, collaborators and, indeed, enemies shapes every human person on the road to adulthood. None of us can escape, nor would we want to escape, the impact and richness of these influences. The best of interpersonal relationships gives beauty and meaning, challenge and purpose to each of our lives—as they did to Jesus' life. And even when a relationship fails, it still can strengthen our resolve to remain faithful, the way Jesus remained faithful when he encountered conflict and betrayal. That's the nature of the interpersonal dimension of life.

It is clear that the personal dimension of life affects our relationship with God. It did for Jesus—it does for us. We relate to God as individuals. It's easy for people of faith to see the connections between this personal, intimate, me-centered dimension of our lives and our spirituality. Almost the entire religious education of Catholics for generations has centered on each one's personal response to God, the individual's specific duties to God, personal faithfulness to God. For centuries Catholic-Christian spirituality has concentrated on the personal dimension of life. This is fine but one-dimensional.

More recently the interpersonal dimension of life has come into focus as a strong force in our spirituality. The crucial influences in our lives of parents, family, friends, teachers, mentors, the example of great people whom we've known or heard about, and even the challenges of less-than-healthy and even flat-out-bad relationships—that entire network of the others whom we know in the course of life—all form part of *our* life in God, *our* spirituality (the plural here is all important). It's clear that we are not alone on life's journey, and we're not supposed to be. Practically the first thing Jesus did as his ministry unfolded was to invite collaborators to join him. And when he was asked for a way to pray, Jesus told us to say, *"Our* Father." We realize that the inter-personal dimension of life is crucial to our spirituality.

Finally, a third dimension of life comes to our attention when we look at the full meaning of God's becoming human. This is the social dimension. Just like Jesus, each of us is born into a particular historical context. Like him, we are of a certain time period, a specific geographical area; we take our place in a people that has a past and a present. There are forces surrounding every one of us that shape our lives for better or for worse: family, neighborhood, housing, education, socio-economic realities, civic government, religious traditions. This was true for Jesus, and it's true for every person born into this world.

I'll never forget when this social dimension of life forced its way into my consciousness. It happened because of hard questions like the one asked by the sister-nurse that evening in Lima and because I was having firsthand experiences of what she was talking about. The poor were all around me, and I could see that no amount of kindly charitable outreach to them was going to change their imprisoned, subhuman lives. Their relationships, too, suffered from the impoverishment of their lives. How many times I witnessed the fabric of a family tear apart because the father despaired of being able to provide for its material needs, the mother taking on the burden of scraping enough money together for daily survival, and the children left pretty much on their own. Society was stacked against them. The terrible social dimension of their lives held them in their oppressed place.

What was almost completely new to me in those days was the absolutely essential place these social realities held in living a truly gospel spirituality. Coming to understand the structures of society that unavoidably shape each of us, I came to realize that we do not live our lives in God only on the plane of the personal and interpersonal. The social dimension of life, which is as close to us as our nationality or cultural background, continues to influence every one of us and is also beyond our individual control, at least in the short run. The social dimension shows itself in social structures such as unequal educational opportunities, in institutionalized and organizational realities like the freedom (or not) for workers to unionize, in networks of laws and customs and priorities like due process before the law in each person's nation and culture. And the social dimension of life stands under a gospel judgment; it stands as a challenge for each person of faith and good will. People are helped or hurt by social realities and, I realized, a true spirituality has to be aware of this fact. Whether I was right or wrong, I came to believe that this social dimension was the most significant reality in the life of Jesus. His consistent response to the historical, and often unjust, structures of his time and place stands as a major thrust in his life and ministry and turned out to be the principal reason for his capture, torture, and death.

What an impact this realization, once gained, makes on the person of faith who lives in the world's only superpower! The consequences of decisions made in places like the White House, Congress, and the Pentagon by a government that is purportedly of us the people, by us the people, and for us the people should shake us to our foundations; it should affect, too, the way we live our faith. In our names the United States strides across the world shaping and reshaping whole societies in its own image and likeness. Terms like "spreading democracy," "combating terrorism," and "extending freedom" too often camouflage an arrogance and brutality that are startling. The disastrous war against Iraq serves as the most recent and glaring example of the empire at work in the world today.

In succeeding chapters we'll return time and again to the consequences of taking seriously not only the personal and interpersonal aspects of our lives and their connection with spirituality, but also, and much more important, the social dimension of our life in God. Not to do so would to my mind fall sinfully short of a full spirituality in a place and time—the United States today—that challenge us mightily as we try to follow Jesus.

Conclusions

We began to think about all these things when our parish team took on the sister-nurse's dilemma that night in Lima. The process of unpacking her crucial question about God's presence in the desperate lives of the impoverished people there went on for a long time—years really—and, at least for me, continues as a work in progress. I'm sure that coming to understand what the incarnation of God means in the light of human suffering and degradation takes a lifetime. But two further and surprising conclusions came to us back then and serve as fitting conclusions to this chapter.

First, we came to one further "answer" to the question the sister posed about where evidence of God exists in the lives of the sick and poor among us. It's in us. If believing in God's incarnation sheds light on that question, further clarity comes when we realize that it is we ourselves who are the evidence today of God's providence—or, we're not. Back then we came to the challenging insight that the whole purpose of the incarnation—of God-with-us—has become the task of all the people who believe in it and act on it, whether explicitly or implicitly. Jesus has left the scene. It's now just us, left, as the Fourth Eucharistic Prayer puts it, to "complete His work on earth." Put negatively, if we are not vitally concerned about the worth of each person, the consequences of each relationship, and the effects of each structure, then to that extent the Incarnate Jesus is absent today.

We saw that people who reach out to other people, especially to those in most need; people who try to make even difficult relationships work; people who beat their heads and fists against the walls of unjust social systems—these are the hands and feet and smile, the healing action, and yes, the saving death of Jesus today. Jesus said all of this quite simply when he prayed: "[Father,] I do not ask you to take them out of the world. . . . As you have sent me into the world, so I have sent them into the world" (Jn 17:15, 18).

A second "answer" to where evidence of God is in human suffering came to us thanks to the poor themselves. We began to look at them in a new way, noticing that they identified with an incarnate God who also suffered—especially on the cross. We saw that they took a great deal of consolation from that aspect of his life. They related to the suffering God of Good Friday much better than to the triumphant God of Easter Sunday. The crucifixion came much closer to their experience than the resurrection.

In fact, we began to see that for us, the non-poor, just the opposite was true. We related more to Easter than to Good Friday.

Since then, I've noticed that very often Christians in the United States begin to wish each other a happy Easter right after the Palm Sunday ceremonies, or surely when the Holy Thursday liturgy has finished. We seem to skip over Good Friday, perhaps because, unlike the poor, our society has rarely had the sort of searing experiences of suffering that they have on a daily basis. This is really an ominous situation for people of faith in the heart of the empire.

And so, our question back in Lima—Where is the evidence of a loving God in the lives of the sick and poor?—had further light shed on it thanks to the example of those same poor and often miserable human beings. They knew a God who shared their pain in the life, especially in the sufferings and death of Jesus. They became truly our teachers. They showed us the way to a realistic spirituality based on what the church there was calling for: a preferential option for the poor. Thanks to those desperately poor, marginalized, oppressed women and men, we came to understand a little better what Jesus the Christ, the incarnation of a loving God, means when, surprisingly, he says to us "as often as you did it—or not—for one of these, the least of my sisters or brothers you did it—or not—for me" (Mt 25:40).

Can we even begin to hope that the same conversion will happen in our country? The poor still have to ability to teach us, to hold out the possibility that we Americans of faith and those of good will can change the course of our history, even now, and begin to serve the impoverished peoples of our nation and the world rather than go on exploiting them. If there is any hope for this empire, I believe it's with people of faith and good will here who "have the eyes to see," who understand the full dimensions of God's incarnation and who act on that understanding.

Chapter 2

• • • • •

Political Reading of the Scriptures

The experience of returning to the United States after working fifteen years in pastoral ministries overseas brought with it
the experience of what people call reverse culture shock. It was
one thing to go off to Latin America and move through all of the
usual struggles, discomforts, and embarrassments involved in
getting used to new ways of doing things—stumbling along while
learning a new language; being confused by very different social
norms; having one's convictions jarred by unfamiliar religious
customs without a clue to their meaning; and as a result feeling
awkward and out of place during the first many months and
beyond. That sort of culture shock was expected as part of the
territory for all of us expatriates, and little by little most of us
negotiated it with varying degrees of grace and comfort.

But despite the fact that I had visited the United States from
time to time during my years overseas, to experience many of
these same discomforts now that I was back to stay in my own
society, among people I thought I knew, took me by surprise and
proved enormously troubling. I understood the language here, I
moved around in familiar surroundings—but after fifteen years
away it was all so different. Another culture shock overtook me,
and I was shocked indeed.

Sometimes it was some little, almost silly example that brought
me up short. I remember being in one of our Franciscan houses
shortly after coming back and watching with increasing irritation
while a brother friar pulled five, six, seven sheets of paper tow-
els from a rack to wipe his hands. Where did my upset come

from, I wondered. What was wrong with me? On reflection, I remembered that back in Peru for a whole series of economic and political reasons we had a lot of difficulty getting enough writing paper for the children in our parish school. And here was an American—a Franciscan yet—using what seemed to me excessive amounts of paper just to dry his hands. There was some logic behind my annoyance, but its intensity in such a trivial matter surprised me.

Another fit of reverse culture shock came during my first Christmas back in the United States. I dreaded its approach and did my best simply to survive the run-up to December 25 with the incessant, media-driven drumbeat, urging everyone to shop and buy, buy and shop that marks that season in our society. This reaction was more understandable but just as disconcerting. It was a bad Christmas for me, and I wondered to myself if I would ever be able to live in my own culture again.

The one thing that gave me the most trouble back here, however, was of quite another type. As I began to get into ministry once again, I felt major upset at what I felt to be an incomplete reading and preaching of the scriptures. In listening to sermons, attending retreat conferences, getting theological updating, it seemed to me that the scriptures were never given their full scope. Preachers, teachers, and retreat directors invariably limited themselves to the personal and sometimes the interpersonal applications of God's word. The social, structural, and political realities of this First World never came in for attention and explanation. This oversight or just plain neglect of such important issues nearly drove me crazy.

During my years overseas it had become like second nature to read the scriptures in a way that always, but *always,* included their social applications. This came from a kind of natural gift for reflection that Latin Americans seem to have embedded in their DNA. And the church there, especially as its liberation theology developed, nurtured in all of us—laity, religious, priests, and bishops—the habit of social analysis and theological reflection when breaking open biblical texts. It became for me the natural, instinctive way of thinking about, praying over, preaching, and teaching God's word, because we did it at every level of church life from the base communities all the way to bishops' meetings. Once I became accustomed to seeing the social applications in virtually every passage of the scriptures, I couldn't read them any other way.

I remembered being at a meeting of the Peruvian Episcopal Conference and being assigned to a small group that included the cardinal of Lima and a factory worker—not an unusual configuration in the Latin American church at that time. In the conversation the young worker shared his experience of a Christmas Eve in the factory when a group of workers took time out to read together the story of Jesus' birth from Luke's Gospel, then shared some bread and wine, as he said, "in remembrance of the newborn Savior." For us who were listening, it was the story of the shepherds near Bethlehem all over again. I remember that the cardinal told the young man that if an opportunity like that ever presented itself again, he had permission to go to a local church and bring the Eucharist to his co-workers.

So it was, and still is, extremely difficult and disconcerting for me not to find back here in the United States what we in Latin America commonly called "a political reading of the gospel." Perhaps the reader can understand how deeply I feel about this when I say that one of my main reasons for returning to this country was to tell the stories about Latin America. I figured that they would immediately resonate here. So, to come back and hear God's word applied almost exclusively in personalized, individualistic ways surprised and bothered me. Could people here ever connect with the richness of that spiritual life we experienced in the South, I wondered. Because to connect with that experience struck me then, as it does now, as very important for North American people of faith—crucial, really, for us who live in a country that has such an impact on the rest of the world. Actually, I have never gotten over this yearning for us in America to give the word of God its fullest scope. Paradoxically, it has remained to this day a welcome part of my reverse culture shock. I'm glad that I've not lost a passion for the "political reading of the gospel" that I brought back with me.

A Full Reading of the Scriptures

That very personal reflection provides a kind of springboard to some examples of the scriptures read in a political way and why we in our First World need to read the scriptures that way. First, however, I have to say that the phrase "political reading of the gospel," used so frequently and understood so well in Latin America, needs some explaining here. It has nothing to do with particular and debatable opinions people might have around specific issues, and nothing to do with partisan politics and objectives. There's nothing in this about Democrat or Republican agendas. Neither is a political reading of the gospel in any way a bending or manipulating of God's word to sway the various, sometimes contradictory choices that people of good will make on any given issue. *Political* in the sense we used it in Latin America and used herein has to do with its root meaning—it comes from the Latin word *polis,* "the life of the people." Very simply, a political reading of the scriptures means the way biblical texts focus on, illuminate, and question the structures of societies and their impact on the lives of human beings.

The great liberation theologian Gustavo Gutiérrez puts it this way: "Things political are not only those which one attends to during the free time afforded by his private life; nor are they even a well-defined area of human existence. The construction . . . of the 'polis,' of a society in which people can live in solidarity, is a dimension which encompasses and severely conditions all of man's activity."[1] This dimension, which in Gutierrez's words "encompasses all [human] activity," is how I'm using the word *political* here. A political reading of the gospel is done especially and above all with social frameworks clearly in mind. Reading scripture politically, of course, does not exhaust the way we receive God's word. The scriptures hold enormous meaning for every one of us individually and for all of us interpersonally. But biblical texts also need to be stretched further to question every structure as it affects the lives of women and men, particularly the poor. That's political.

The New Testament

Parable of the Talents

The best way to understand what it means to read the scriptures politically is actually to do it. One very good example of extending God's word to include a fuller—political—application comes out of Jesus' parable of the talents in Luke 19. We know the story well. It tells of three people who get varying sums of money from their employer. Two of them use theirs profitably, and one hides his out of fear. The usual reading of this parable invites us to look at ourselves and ask how we as individuals are using what God has given us. Are we putting to good use our God-given gifts like intelligence and health and emotional well-being, and our acquired gifts like money or position or power? Good questions for people of faith in this world of wealth and privilege. However, there's much more to the lesson that Jesus wanted to teach, I think, when we read the parable politically.

For example, what about the countless numbers of people in our world who never get a chance to use their gifts? What about the hungry, uneducated, impoverished masses of human beings today whose gifts through no fault of their own will forever lie hidden because they never got the opportunity to use them? In this political/social reading of the parable, isn't there a challenge to us, who get so many opportunities to use our talents? Aren't we under a gospel imperative to make sure other human beings get to use theirs as well? And doesn't it question a society that increasingly promotes the well-being of people who are already doing pretty well, while neglecting the ones at the bottom of the social ladder? Think of what happened in New Orleans when Hurricane Katrina devastated that city and which segment of the population continues to be left behind.

And that quickly brings us to another insight the parable can give us—another political reading. What about those "acquired" talents of ours? How did we get our money, or our social position in life, or the power we exercise? Isn't it possible that an unbalanced socio-economic system allowed us to rise on the backs of poor people? It's almost a cliché today to say that in global terms the wealth of the world has been flowing from the poor to the rich for decades now. A quick look at the debts owed by poor countries to national and international lending institutions proves the point. So we who live under the umbrella of those institutions and make out very well within this skewed economic calculus find ourselves questioned by this deeper (political) look at this reading.

Going a bit further along this line, we're invited by the parable to examine the reasons why the talents of so many human beings lie hidden, never used. It's rarely due to poor people's laziness or lack of initiative, even though powerful people often use those phantasms when they speak and legislate about poverty. The poor are poor mainly because of readily understandable social systems that favor some at the expense of many. Economic, racial, and gender inequities are too often crucial threads in the fabric of national and international life. Again, the Katrina experience in our country proves the point. Remember who got left behind both during the hurricane and in the months that followed.

I once heard a politician in Peru use the parable of the talents to make the same point. He told about a famous Peruvian tennis player, Alex Olmeda, who performed brilliantly for the U.S. Davis Cup tennis teams during the 1950s. According to the story, Alex was the son of a groundskeeper at an exclusive tennis club in Arequipa, Peru's second largest city. Part of the elder Olmeda's job was to volley with patrons of the club as they prepared for their matches, and he became quite good at it. When young Alex came along, he would go to the club with his father, and eventually he too began hitting tennis balls back and forth with club members. An American businessman happened to visit the club on one occasion and, as he watched the boy volleying on the court, saw that he had a real talent for tennis. Eventually, Alex was brought to this country, got an education and coaching, and became a star—for the United States!—in international competition. At the conclusion of this happy-ending story the politician asked the hard question: "How many more Alex Olmedas are there in Peru today? How many boys and girls live here whose natural gifts will never be discovered and developed?" As I remember it, the candidate made the connection with this parable. A political reading.

When we read it this way, Jesus' call for each human being to make use of, and indeed to multiply what he or she has received, echoes around the world and questions everything that keeps a majority from doing just that. And fear can't be allowed to hold us back from doing the right thing and making sure that everyone gets a chance at full human development. Too many times we've heard excuses—"if we raise their salaries, the profits will collapse," or "we've got to cut social spending," or "only the 'deserving' poor should get help." The fear of losing comfort, security, and the good life in the face of legitimate demands for basic justice toward the poor is bogus or, as Jesus called it, useless. There's plenty of this world's goods for everyone, if the people and societies on the top stop taking much, much more than a fair share.

Read this way the demands of the parable of the talents jump off the page at us. They go a long way past the simple, almost simplistic question: am I using my talents well?

Matthew 25

Another very good example of reading the gospel in a political way is found in the amazing story of the Last Judgment in Matthew 25. Just like the previous parable, this passage is familiar and challenging to us on a personal level. Jesus tells us that the basis for God's judgment of our lives won't be religious activities and practices—the number of prayers we've said, how many church services we've attended, how much self-denial or penances we've practiced. He says that the determining factors will be what we did or did not do for the hungry, thirsty, unknown, naked, sick, and imprisoned human beings who came across our path in life. He even goes further to say, astoundingly, that what we did or did not do for these "least of the brothers and sisters" was or was not done for him.

The personal application of how we'll be judged is obvious and traditional. We know that we have to make sure to pay attention to and to serve the needy. This is the way we've always read it. It's really a bedrock conviction for every serious person of faith. However, looking at this portion of Matthew's Gospel in political terms pushes it ever so much further. Some examples of reading Matthew 25 politically:

"I was hungry"—often people in our world go hungry and even starve to death because governments don't have the will to get available food out to where it's needed—those are policy choices.

"I was thirsty"—human beings in poor areas of the world increasingly find clean water too scarce and too expensive, or often they have to put up with polluted water because some company has saved money by dumping its waste into local streams and rivers—those are economic questions.

"I was a stranger and you received me"—the stranger is not only the person who might need directions or a place to stay in one of our large cities; he or she is among the millions of refugees who roam across the planet without a place to call home, often turned away from countries like the United States—that is a national and international issue.

"I was naked and you clothed me"—to be naked doesn't only mean to be walking around in rags; it describes, for example, deinstitutionalized mental patients who stand defenseless (naked) on street corners—that's a policy of social engineering.

"I was sick and you comforted me"—too many people languish and die because health insurance is denied them—a human rights question.

"I was in prison and you came to visit me"—the hungry and thirsty, the strangers, the naked, the sick are invariably imprisoned within the walls of national and international policies like the free-market system or the NAFTAs and CAFTAs of international trade, to name just two. The words of Jesus in Matthew 25 question the very foundation of those policies and trade agreements that favor the "haves" over the "have nots." That is a political and I think very necessary reading of Matthew 25, particularly for people of faith and good will in the United States today. As a nation we are not moving in the right direction. Those negative political decisions just mentioned are becoming more and more common in this country as the twenty-first century unfolds.

For ten years an African American grandmother lived next door to our inner-city community house in Washington DC. Ms. Virginia was one of those typical, strong matriarchs in the black community who often hold their children and grandchildren together as family through the sheer force of their will. She was also unwell, suffering from chronic heart disease, arthritis, and cancer, and was not able to work outside her home. When successive presidential administrations sliced social spending in the 1980s and 1990s, and the "welfare queens" were ordered to go out and get jobs, Ms. Virginia told us one day that if those policies kept up, she and her little ones would lose their food stamps and literally go hungry. Matthew's account of the Last Judgment, if we read it politically, encompasses those situations and their causes.

The Magnificat

Mary's prayer as related in Luke 2:46–55 would startle us with its political language, if we could really hear it. The context for the prayer is dramatic and so very human. The young woman from Nazareth hurries up into the hill country to help out an elderly cousin, Elizabeth, whose own unexpected pregnancy is proof of the archangel's promise that she, Mary, will mother the Messiah. At the doorway of Elizabeth's home, when she hears the older woman's inspired greeting, "Blessed are you among women," Mary lifts up a beautiful poem of praise to the God who has done great things for her, whose name is holy and whose mercy stretches from generation to generation.

Then comes the startling part. Mary goes on to glorify God's strength in "scattering the proud in the thoughts of their hearts . . . bringing down the powerful from their thrones and lifting up the lowly . . . filling the hungry with good things and sending the rich away empty." It doesn't take much imagination to connect Mary's understanding of God's "political" action to all sorts of realities in today's world, beginning with our own country. We know who are the proud, the powerful. Just think of the decision-makers in the U.S. State Department, the White House, and the Pentagon. We know why God would "scatter them, bring them down, send them away." We know who are the lowly and the hungry and why God would "lift them up and fill them with good things." An attentive (political) reading of that part of the Magnificat shows Mary's prayer as downright revolutionary. Her God has definite preferences; God has a preferential option for the poor. The prayer also turns a searchlight on the world of power and pride that is the United States.

Political Readings from the Hebrew Scriptures

The Hebrew scriptures also include the same political reading one can see in New Testament texts. The Exodus story, which tells about God's intervention in the liberation of an oppressed people, stands as the model and inspiration for every human struggle aimed at throwing off slavery and moving toward freedom. We can read this biblical epic in personal terms—each one's efforts to overcome the addictions and dependencies that stand in his or her way to fuller humanity. We can read it in its interpersonal dimension—remaining faithful in our relationships and allowing them to nurture us into ongoing and ever deeper humanness. And with the eyes to see, we cannot help but read Exodus in a political way—discerning who are the pharaohs of our times, what are the roadblocks, and what are the idols that hold entire populations back from true liberation and development.

I once had a firsthand experience of an Exodus event in the lives of an imprisoned people. During the years of war in El Salvador over the decade of the 1980s, large numbers of peasants were driven off their lands and sought sanctuary in neighboring Honduras. After ten miserable years in a camp called Mesa Grande, one such refugee population of about five thousand people decided to return home to El Salvador and, despite the continuing conflict there, begin their lives over again. They felt that life back on their own land would be far better than continuing to languish in exile. These brave people invited a number of us as international observers/protectors to accompany them on their risky journey back to El Salvador.

I went to Mesa Grande and saw the story of the Exodus lived out again, and very consciously, by these simple folk. They knew their Bible, and they had a sense of the striking coincidence between what they were doing and what the Hebrew nation had done centuries before. In fact, at one point in the process of returning home the Salvadoran government threatened to close the border against them, and the refugees hesitated. They gathered two days before the scheduled departure and read the book of Exodus—then decided to go ahead with their return.

As it turned out their passage—their exodus—from the slave-like situation of that refugee camp to freedom back on their own lands proved successful. I remember hearing a Honduran military official order his troops to stand aside as the Salvadorans set out for home. The Red Sea parted. Church people in El Salvador met us at the border and welcomed these brothers and sisters back home. Pharaoh was thwarted. The refugees made it home and took up the threads of their lives once again. It's not impossible to imagine that, just like the ancient People of the Book, those Salvadoran peasants will honor their "Passover" for generations to come. "There shall you eat the Passover sacrifice, in the evening at sunset, the time of day when you departed from Egypt" (Dt 16:6).

U.S. Americans can profitably read Exodus in a political way. A strong case can be made that as a society we are the modern version of Egyptian overlords. A glance at our immigration policies and how we too often mistreat the newcomers among us proves the point. The phrases of poet Emma Lazarus, carved for the world to see on the Statue of Liberty in New York harbor, seem almost laughable today:

> Give me your tired, your poor,
> Your huddled masses yearning to breathe free,
> The wretched refuse of your teeming shore.
> Send these, the homeless, tempest-tossed to
>   me,
> I lift my lamp beside the golden door!

Our immigration laws no longer reflect those generous words. Instead, the first words of Exodus describe the situation of people migrating to the United States now: "Look how numerous and powerful the Israelite [immigrant] people are growing, more so than we ourselves! Come let us deal shrewdly with them to stop their increase. . . . Accordingly, taskmasters were set over the Israelites [undocumented] to oppress them with forced labor. . . . The Egyptians [Americans], then, dreaded the Israelites [immigrants] and reduced them to cruel slavery, making life bitter for them with hard work in mortar and brick and all kinds of field work—the whole cruel fate of slaves" (Ex 1:8–14). So, this early and paradigmatic story of a people's move from slavery to freedom stands as a severe indictment of the United States and our treatment of "huddled masses yearning to breathe free."

Prophets' Word

The prophetic tradition in the Hebrew scriptures is overwhelmingly political as well. Texts from Isaiah, Jeremiah, and Amos illustrate the point:

"What to me is the multitude of your sacrifices? Says the Lord . . . cease to do evil, learn to do good: seek justice, rescue the oppressed, defend the orphan, plead for the widow" (Is 1:11,17). We often congratulate ourselves that U.S. churches are full on Sundays. But are we as a people, and especially our representative government, seriously concerned about the oppressed, the orphans, or the widows in this country and around the world? In recent presidential campaigns in this country it was almost impossible to find any mention of wealth and poverty here, or across the globe. And yet Isaiah tells us that our society, like all others, will be judged on concern for those left out, not on church attendance, on the "multitude of sacrifices."

"For from the least to the greatest of them, everyone is greedy for unjust gain; and from prophet to priest, everyone deals falsely. They have treated the wound of my people carelessly saying, 'Peace, peace,' when there is no peace" (Jer 6: 13–14). Jeremiah's words on God's behalf, questioning all claims to peace when there is none, resound in a world where war-making is often called "the right to sovereignty," in our country which justifies an obscene nuclear-weapons stockpile as "safeguards of national security," and at a time when even the scarce treasure of countless societies bleeds away in the production and purchase of arms. "The wound of my people" that Jeremiah speaks about is left to fester when, as the saying goes, guns replace butter.

"I will restore the fortunes of my people . . . and they shall rebuild the ruined cities and inhabit them; they shall plant vineyards and drink their wine, and they shall make gardens and eat their fruit. I will plant them upon their land, and they shall never again be plucked up out of the land that I have given them, says

the Lord your God" (Am 9:14–15). The vision in Amos of homeless people who finally get to rebuild their own cities and drink
the wine of the vineyards they plant brings to mind the Salvadorans mentioned above—and Palestinians, Iraqis, Rwandans,
Sudanese, former residents of New Orleans, and indigenous
peoples everywhere today. They yearn and struggle for the promise held out by Prophet Amos long ago. As a matter of fact, I
know of another Salvadoran group that actually read and reread
the following passage as it took leave of its refugee camp and traveled home over landmined roads in a war zone of that country:

> "Yes, the days are coming," says the Lord,
> "When the plowman shall overtake the reaper,
> And the vintager, him who sows the seed;
> The juice of grapes shall drip down the
>   mountains,
> And all the hills shall run with it.
> I will bring about the restoration of my people
>   Israel;
> They shall rebuild and inhabit their ruined cities,
> Plant vineyards and drink the wine,
> Set out gardens and eat the fruits.
> I will plant them upon their own ground;
> Never again shall they be plucked
> From the land I have given them, say I, the Lord,
>   your God." (Am 9:13–15)

These are just samplings of the incredibly rich prophetic tradition of the Hebrew scriptures, but they are enough to point up
the complex and challenging connections between the political
message of the prophets centuries ago and various oppressions
and neglect that confront whole peoples and countries today.[2]

The Jubilee Tradition and the Psalms

Jubilee

   One remarkable example of how God's word questions human
systems and structures spans both the Hebrew scriptures and the

New Testament. The Jubilee tradition is God's continual call for a restoration of right relationships—personal, interpersonal, and social—explicitly laid out in Leviticus 25: "You shall hallow the fiftieth year and you shall proclaim liberty throughout the land to all its inhabitants. It shall be a jubilee for you: you shall return, every one of you, to your property and every one of you to your family" (v. 10). Then God goes on to detail what goes into a full repair of personal and social arrangements that have gotten skewed: freeing slaves, forgiving debts, retrieving property, letting the land lie fallow.

Earlier in the Exodus story God teaches the Jubilee mentality of being content with what is enough for daily living: "Then the Lord said to Moses, 'I am going to rain bread from heaven for you, and each day the people shall go out and gather enough for that day'" (Ex 16:4).

Centuries later, Jesus' own prayer echoes that same Jubilee attitude: "Give us each day our daily bread" (Lk 11:3).

In Mark's Gospel the Jubilee mystique of enough for everyone shows through the parable of the sower. In a society where a sevenfold yield was about enough for a farmer to survive for another year, Jesus says: "Some seed, finally, landed on good soil and yielded grain that sprang up to produce at a rate of thirty—and sixty—and a hundredfold" (Mk 4:8).

It is not hard to make political applications of these texts in a world where mergers and conglomerates and monopolies are the order of the day; where the number of billionaires keeps on growing; where no degree of personal and national security ever seems enough; and where people complain of "charity fatigue"—hearing too much about the needs of whole populations that lack basics like food, water and medicine.[3]

As the world came up on a new millennium in the decade of the 1990s, Pope John Paul II began to anticipate 2000 as "the Year of the Great Jubilee." In his World Day of Peace Message on January 1, 1998, the pope said, "The Jubilee of the Year 2000 is fast approaching. . . . In the biblical tradition it was also a time for freeing slaves, for returning land to its rightful owner, for forgiving debts, thus restoring the conditions of equality willed by God among all the members of the people. It is therefore a special time for seeking that justice which leads to peace." He also had this to say about what Jubilee means in a modern context: "My thoughts go here to one of the greatest difficulties which the poorer nations have to face today. I refer to the heavy burden of external debt, which compromises the economies of whole peoples and hinders their social and political progress." John Paul was reading Jubilee in political/economic terms.

During that same decade of the 1990s thousands of other faith-filled and good-willed people also saw in the Jubilee ideal a way to spark efforts to lift from the backs of poor societies the crushing external debt that governments, their own and others, and international lending institutions had laid on them. While this movement ultimately fell short of its ambitious goal of restoring basic equity (a right relationship) between debtor countries and powerful institutions that hold them in financial bondage, it can be hoped that the Jubilee vision will endure, thanks to the wonderful people who see its application to our world—people who, like John Paul II, read it politically.

The Psalms

If we look and really see, there are clusters of psalms that are political and applicable in very pointed ways to modern realities, especially when read from the point of view of people who suffer war, hunger, and poverty—and from the point of view of societies that inflict these evils on others.

What can we U.S. Americans say about the Iraq war when we hear Psalm 5: "You are not a God who delights in wickedness; evil will not sojourn with you. The boastful will not stand before your eyes; you hate evildoers. You destroy those who speak lies; the Lord abhors the bloodthirsty and deceitful."

How do people of privilege feel when we imagine oppressed peoples praying Psalm 36: "Do not let the foot of the arrogant tread on me, or the hand of the wicked drive me away. There the evildoers lie prostrate; they are thrust down, unable to rise."

Shouldn't the First World take notice of Psalm 80 and its plea to God on behalf of today's "underdeveloped" societies: "O Lord, God of hosts, how long will you be angry with your people's prayers? You have fed them with the bread of tears, and given them tears to drink in full measure. . . . Restore us, O God of hosts."

Catholic Social Teaching and the Scriptures

Catholic social teaching finds its grounding on a political reading of biblical texts. In his wonderful 1967 social encyclical, *On the Development of Peoples*, Pope Paul VI talks about the scandalous gap between privilege and deprivation in today's world: "The point at issue is the establishment of a human society in which everyone regardless of race, religion or nationality can live a truly human life free from the bondage imposed by men and the forces of nature not sufficiently mastered; a society in which freedom is not an empty word and where *Lazarus, the poor man, can sit at the same table as the rich man*" (emphasis added) (no. 47).

This is a reading of a gospel text to make a point about social (political) justice. Pope Paul VI is saying that Jesus' parable applies to the global realities of wealth versus poverty, just as much as it applies to the personal concern each of us ought to have for the "Lazarus" who might approach us on a street corner or come to our door for a handout. Pope John Paul II made a similar point with the same gospel story, but, typically for him, in a more direct way, on one of his visits to the United States. He told us "Lazarus is at your gate," which was a strict warning to the developed world. As we remember, the whole point of this parable is that the sin of the rich man is not so much in his wealth (Jesus had some things to say about the rich in another place) but in the fact that he ignores the poor Lazarus who sits day after day at his gate covered with sores.

On a Sunday morning years ago in Lima I learned a lesson about Lazarus at the gate. A wealthy banker came up to me after one of the Masses and asked me where were all these poor people I spoke about so often in my homilies. I took the man to a place near where he lived and showed him the pathetic hovel where an impoverished family was living. Every day the banker left his lovely home and passed that place in his air-conditioned Mercedes automobile, but he never saw these Lazaruses at his gate.

Catholic social teaching is above all an ethic of life. So the great challenge from God to the Israelites in the book of Deuteronomy—"I have set before you life and death, blessings and

curses. Choose life so that you and your descendants may live"
(Dt 30:19)—clearly undergirds the church's insistence that we
opt for life at its every stage, from before birth through natural
death. Peace is a constant theme of Catholic social teaching.
Isaiah's prophecy "they shall beat their swords into plowshares,
and their spears into pruning hooks; nation shall not lift up
sword against nation, neither shall they learn war any more" (Is
2:4) underscores this theme and its call for nonviolent ways to
settle local, national, and international disputes. Catholic social
teaching is concerned with human rights. It finds inspiration in
the famous line from Micah 6, "What does the Lord require of
you but to do justice, and to love kindness, and to walk humbly
with your God." Those telling phrases clearly motivate broad
efforts like those of Bread for the World to feed hungry populations (do justice), and all the work done by groups like Amnesty
International on behalf of human rights (love kindness), and the
rejection of the modern idols of wealth, power, and security that
the Catholic Worker movement lives out (walk humbly with your
God).

The references to the Bible in Catholic social teaching go on
and on. Jesus' observation in Matthew 6:21 "where your treasure
is there is your heart" shines a light on the scandal of extreme
wealth and extreme poverty that exist side by side in our world.
The story of the rich young man in Mark 10:17–21 and Jesus'
call for him to give all to the poor is echoed in our church's stern
message to rich neighborhoods, rich societies, and the rich northern half of the planet. Here are the words of Pope Paul VI, writing in the encyclical letter *A Call to Action,* on this same subject:
"The Gospel instructs us in the preferential respect due the poor
and the special situation they have in society; *the more fortunate
should renounce some of their rights so as to place their goods more
generously at the service of others*" (emphasis added) (no. 23).

When God's word gets expanded to embrace social (political)
realities, the church itself comes under scrutiny. Catholic social
teaching has to be applied to the scandal of excessive wealth in
church organizations from the Vatican to religious orders to suburban parishes; to the scandal of how the church treats women;
to union-busting on the part of dioceses; to the fact that most of
us in the U.S. church enjoy lives of privilege, while the majority
of our sisters and brothers across the world is destitute. The in-

sights and directions of Catholic social teaching, based on scripture, have to be applied above all to the scandal of pedophile and predator priests and its coverup by those bishops who showed themselves more interested in the institution than in their people. Pope Paul VI said it clearly in *A Call to Action:* "It is not enough to recall principles, state intentions, point to crying injustices and utter prophetic denunciations; these words will lack real weight unless they are accompanied for each individual by a livelier awareness of personal responsibility and by effective action" (no. 48).

The ideal of the first Christian communities to hold everything in common (Acts 2:43–47; 5:12–16) is repeated in many of the church's social documents that speak of core values like solidarity, the common good, respect for the dignity of individuals, and the burning issues of international debt, consumerism, and private property. Our church has a long way to go in living up to the social implications of biblical texts. We don't even hear much of this crucial political take on God's word from our pulpits at a time when the United States desperately needs to hear it. It is a well-kept secret.

In Chapter 5, on obedience, I'll come back to the nexus between Catholic social teaching and an engaged spirituality. Let me just say here that this "well-kept secret" in our faith tradition has everything to do today with building a scripture-based, mission-oriented spirituality. One quote from Catholic social teaching, out of hundreds that I could choose, makes this point with startling clarity: "Action on behalf of justice and participation in the transformation of the world fully appear to us as *constituitive [essential] to the preaching of the gospel*" (emphasis added).[4] If I read it correctly, the bishops flatly state that justice and transforming the world stand with the Eucharist and God's word at the very center of Christian living today. How can spirituality, lived in the heart of an empire that has such an impact on the rest of the world, ignore anything so clear?

Conclusion

It must be clear from everything I've written here that I find it impossible not to see God's word in political as well as personal terms. For me, the entire Bible makes a social statement, as well as inspiring personal and interpersonal conversion. Jesus' own involvement in the social realities of his time is clearly antici- pated throughout the Hebrew scriptures and shines through vir- tually every page of the Christian scriptures. In light of this, a real spirituality has to focus outward as much as inward—perhaps more so. Biblical imperatives simply won't let us turn into our- selves. So while the word of God is given for our personal inspi- ration and benefit, its power inevitably pushes us outward to- ward the larger world around us—if we let it. Reading the scriptures politically is a way to harness that power and keep it alive in each of us.

A final story will put an exclamation point on this chapter. It will also, I hope, highlight what a gift the poor can be to the rest of us in understanding God's word politically. Some years ago I found myself in a remote area of the Peruvian Andes, visiting a sister with whom I had worked in Lima. My time there stretched over a weekend and the local people asked if I would celebrate Sunday Mass with them since they had no resident priest. The sister told me that representatives of base Christian communities from surrounding pueblos gathered for two hours each Sunday to prepare the worship service, and I would be expected to join them.

It happened that the readings for that particular Sunday in- cluded one from the Prophet Jeremiah: "Blessed is the one who trusts in the Lord, whose hope is in the Lord. He is like a tree planted beside the waters that stretches out its roots to the stream: it fears not the heat when it comes, its leaves stay green; In the year of drought it shows no distress but still bears fruit" (Jer 17:7–8). As always, the question these indigenous folks asked was what is the message of the scriptures today. The prob- lem was that over the previous several months a drought had hit that region and there was a good chance that they would not reap much of a harvest that year. In fact, the possibility of widespread hunger loomed large. What could the prophet's words about fruit- ful trees stretching roots out to flowing waters mean in that situ- ation, they asked.

Being semiliterate peasants, these liturgy planners took a long time to read the passage over and over and ponder its meaning for themselves. As we sat there and the minutes ticked by, it seemed clear to me that they would come to a dead end—that nothing of the "tree planted by water, sending out its roots by the stream" could possibly apply to what they were going through. I had nothing to offer; as an outsider, an American coming from a different part of that country, it was not my place to suggest anything. Furthermore, I really had no clue about what the Jeremiah text might mean for these people and their present reality.

But as happened so often in these sorts of situations, after a long time one man timidly spoke up and said: "I think what God's word is saying is that we will have to be the living water for each other. Some people may salvage some of their crops, and they'll have to share what they gather with the others who lose everything." Everyone in the group thought about this and finally agreed—yes, we have to be living water for one another. That has to be the message preached that Sunday. And as I listened, I'm sure with tears in my eyes, I realized that these materially poor women and men were not theorizing. There was nothing abstract about their political reading of Jeremiah; they would share from their need, from their poverty, from their hunger. It was all very real and perhaps the best, most poignant and valid example of a political reading of the scriptures I can ever remember hearing.

What a difference in our church and society this way of reading God's word would make!

Chapter 3

• • • • •

Prayer and Contemplation

A long segment in the first chapter of Mark's Gospel (Mark 1:21:38) has always fascinated me, because it lays out what you might call "a day in the life of Jesus." Mark walks us through a twelve- or fourteen-hour period describing in detail the way our Lord must have moved through the years of his public life. I think, too, that we get a glimpse of Jesus' prayer and surprisingly find it to be much like our own in lots of ways—distracted, interrupted, and very worldly.

Mark places Jesus in the synagogue at Capernaum sometime during the afternoon hours preaching "with authority" (v. 21) to the crowds. It's early in his ministry and the people are just beginning to get a sense that this Teacher is something out of the ordinary—"spellbound" is what Mark says about their reaction to him that day. They bring into the synagogue a person possessed by an "unclean spirit" (v. 23) and suddenly we have one of those highly charged encounters between good and evil which dot the pages of the Gospels. The powers of darkness try to put a name on Jesus: "I know who you are—the holy One of God" (v. 24). If they can do that, then maybe they can win out over him. Energetically, Jesus silences the spirit and drives it out of the man ("He rebuked him sharply: Be quiet and come out of him" [v. 25]). The people sense "a completely new teaching in a spirit of authority" (v. 27).

After that emotional episode Jesus leaves the synagogue and goes with a couple of his friends to the home of Simon Peter, where he finds Simon's mother-in-law in bed with a fever. He gets her back on her feet, and then it seems the whole town shows up at the doorway of the house, bringing the sick and disturbed for his healing touch. This activity apparently stretches far into the evening.

Mark takes up the story early the following morning as Jesus goes off by himself to a lonely place in the desert and is absorbed in prayer (v. 35). But there is still no rest for him. The disciples "track him down" (v. 36) to tell him that he's got to go back to the village where the people are looking for him to help them. Mark closes out this particular narrative by saying that Jesus then decides to move on to "the neighboring villages" (v. 38), where he is called to preach as well.

The sheer busyness of those many hours comes through loud and clear, doesn't it. Jesus has no time to eat or rest throughout that afternoon and into the night. (In Mark 3:21, Mark reports that the Lord's family "comes to take charge of him" because they think the intensity of the work has literally driven him out of his mind.) The energy he put out preaching so compellingly to the crowd on that afternoon in Capernaum, then confronting and dominating an evil spirit, and finally dealing for the rest of the day with all sorts of physical and psychological illnesses—all of it must have taken a heavy toll. In addition, Jesus doesn't reach everyone. He has the frustrating experience of not getting all of the work done. Even when he finally carves out a bit of quiet time for himself early in the morning, they still refuse to leave him alone. "They track him down" and the whole cycle apparently starts over again. Some might call Jesus a workaholic.

It's easy to imagine, too, what Jesus was praying about in the short time he did have that morning. Wouldn't the faces and voices and requests that surrounded him on the day before in the synagogue and at Simon's house crowd in on him as he moved into those brief solitary moments? How could he not have been thinking about, really distracted by, all of what happened just a few hours before? It would be impossible for him, I think, not to have in the forefront of his thoughts all those people he had seen and all the needs he had addressed, and yes, the ones he could not reach the evening before.

It's really consoling to think that Jesus had to accept the fact that a lot of the work in Capernaum would be left undone, at

least for the moment, as he decides to move on to other towns
and villages. The disciples tell him that "everybody is looking for
you" (v. 37), and yet he says they have to push on. All that unfinished business must have formed part of his prayer as well—
he surely brought it to that alone time with his Abba God. Hu-
manly, it couldn't have been otherwise, could it? It's consoling as
well to know that on that occasion and surely on many others
Jesus' prayer was cut short by the demands and expectations of
those around him. It's obvious that Jesus' own prayer was very
much connected with the here and now, full of distractions, and
at least on this occasion cut short.

Prayer of Modern People

That rich reflection on Jesus' extremely active ministry and
his distracted and interrupted prayer resonates with so many of
us today as we try our best to keep God present in our too busy
lives and in our moments of disjointed prayer. It also reminds me
of the statement made by the great twentieth-century theologian
Karl Rahner: modern people of faith pray best with the Bible in
one hand and the daily newspaper in the other. We do need
God's word to inspire and inform our prayer; but that prayer is
best done with our complicated and hurting world very much in
mind. Jesus' prayer, his being "absorbed in God," must have been
influenced by all that went on that day in Capernaum and on so
many similar occasions. Our prayers should have similar influences.

I live in an intentional community in the heart of Washington
DC where each member works to bring about social change. One
teaches in an inner-city Catholic school, another works for
America Corps, another with street people. Doing something to
change society for the better is one of the requirements for mem-
bership in the community. Since we started more than twenty
years ago, the community has taken time early each morning to
pray together in our living room, usually beginning with the
scripture readings of the day. We reflect with one another and ask
God's help about the many issues, problem areas, and people
whose lives cross ours day after day—the problem children of

that inner-city school; solidarity efforts with countries like Haiti, Colombia, and Palestine that several members work at; the struggle of another, a survivor of torture, to abolish that awful reality in our world. Always, always we voice our common yearning for peace and our opposition to solving conflicts through violence—the morning prayer ends with the "Peace Prayer" of St. Francis. We really do pray with the word of God and the daily newspaper in hand; the world and its large and small contexts and the daily scripture readings set the agenda for how our prayer goes each morning.

Even the gritty setting of our two community row houses located in the inner city, the "other Washington," lends itself to this kind of prayer. Local buses rattle past our door and screech to a halt at the stop on the corner; loud, sometimes angry voices penetrate the early morning quiet in that overcrowded and poor neighborhood; once in a while gunshots ring out signaling a drug deal gone bad. And the fact that we live about twenty blocks from the White House, Congress, and the State Department—in the "belly of the beast," the heart of the empire—sparks daily analyses and prayers around the decisions being made in those centers of power. It's not hard to imagine the kind of intercessory prayer we offered when one of our community members, Sister Dianna Ortiz, tried to pry open the government's container of silence around her torture and American complicity in it, or how we prayerfully joined another of our group when she carried out a water-only fast protesting U.S. policies toward Central America, or how we pray when a community member is going to Capitol Hill to give testimony on a human rights issue, or our prayers in solidarity when members do civil disobedience to confront our country's wars in Afghanistan and Iraq.

These "distractions" are the raw material of what we pray about, as I think Jesus' realities must have been for him during his busy and engaged life. Rarely quiet, usually interrupted, hardly satisfying, but genuine prayer nevertheless—for us and for him.

Valuing this sort of preoccupied, noisy, outwardly focused prayer is not what I was taught when I entered the Franciscan Order and began my preparation for religious life and ministry. I don't believe it is what they teach even today in courses and lectures and conferences on different prayer forms. When I look back on my introduction to prayer, my memory is of an introspective, introverted approach—being told to go as deeply as possible within myself to find God. I was supposed to treat competing thoughts as distractions and unhelpful for real prayer and to get them out of my mind. But there I was, a hopeless extrovert, totally aware of cars going by and people talking on the street outside the novitiate chapel, aware of my fellow novices around me inside that sacred space. Why didn't anyone ever tell me that any and all of those externals could be my prayer? Perhaps these memories are faulty or incomplete after so many years, but I do have a clear sense that we were taught approaches to prayer that tried to eliminate extroversion, noisiness, and outside intrusions. It was as if all of us suddenly had to become introverts if we wanted to pray well. In the light of the experiences of Jesus himself—as I try to suggest in this chapter—it does seem that at least equal value should be given to external, worldly, daily-newspaper sorts of inspirations to prayer.

A Different Way of Praying

I'm sure that my one-sided and for me unworkable introduction to prayer was corrected when I came into contact with the wonderful practice of theological reflection in Latin America. The whole church there awakened when the Second Vatican Council, liberation theology, the process of conscientization, and above all, the Medellín Conference all happened in the space of a few short years. It was really a new Pentecost for all of us there at the time. And a significant part of that graced moment was the prayerful, scripture-based reflections done in every area of church life, from the base Christian communities, to parishes, to solidarity groups, to bishops' conferences.

The process of this theological reflection was simple in the extreme. All over Latin America people would come together to do four very doable things: analyze a current situation, read God's word, look at the connections between the situation and scripture, and decide on an action. In the case of those peasants high in the Andean region of Peru that I wrote about at the end of Chapter 2, the situation was a drought, the scripture was a vision of living water, the connection was themselves, and the action was to urge each one to be living water for the others. This cycle of praxis, as it came to be called, always included a concrete situation, social analysis of the situation, theological reflection in the light of God's word, and an agreed-upon action. I found it to be prayer in the best sense. I took to it like a duck to water as it stimulated my extroverted nature and interest in what was going on around me.

I think this outward tilt to prayer ought to apply as well to liturgy, the public prayer of faith communities, and especially to eucharistic celebrations. It applies in a particularly important way to us here in the United States at this point in our history. How can we not connect these two realities—U.S. Catholic-Christians and U.S. citizens? We'll take a whole chapter to look at the "worldly" aspects of Eucharist, but one example here helps to make the point that public prayer needs to be intertwined with public policy.

At the beginning of every Mass, Catholic communities take time for the Rite of Reconciliation, in which we acknowledge once again our need for God's forgiveness ("Let us call to mind our sins"), and then to pray for it ("Lord have mercy"). Shouldn't one important dimension of that need and that prayer move it beyond individual faults and sins, beyond even a particular community's possible divisions or disputes? At that moment of reconciliation, just as we begin the Liturgy of the Word and the Eucharist, it strikes me that the faith community stands as representatives of U.S. American society and has to ask God's forgiveness, mercy and forbearance for the sins of our nation. Leaders of prayer, presiders, and lectors at our eucharistic celebrations need to make this outward, global, worldly dimension of forgiveness quite specific, naming places and issues like the Middle East, Guantanamo, Haiti, free-trade agreements, the war on terrorism, global warming, and so on as areas of our national life that cry out for God's pardon.

Whether it is personal private prayer, interpersonal shared prayer, or communal liturgical prayer, I believe Rahner's insight applies—the word of God in one hand, the daily newspaper in the other. Specific situations in our hurting world, especially those caused by our nation's policies, have to impinge on our "solid moments with the Lord."

Contemplation

Some years ago three friends and I wrote a book called *St. Francis and The Foolishness of God.*[1] It was a reflection on the impact that saint of the thirteenth century has had on the non-poor of modern times. People seemed to get what we were driving at—that Francis of Assisi still continues to question, inspire, and challenge people of good will even eight hundred years after his time. We writers were a mixed group: two men and two women, two married and two single, two Protestants and two Catholics, two ordained ministers and two laity. Our differences seemed to enrich the discussions we had on the various chapters, and the writing went along very well—until we began to write about contemplation.

The two of us who were Catholics felt that contemplation was basically one further dimension of prayer. There are, we said, private and public prayers, individual and communal prayer, liturgical and devotional prayers—and contemplative prayer. All pretty much equal. We thought that contemplation was simply one expression of prayer among many. So, for example, Francis could be found praying with his brothers, with the people around Assisi, with his friend Clare and her sisters, at Mass—and from time to time he would go off to places like the cave at Mount Alverna and get lost for days in contemplative prayer.

One of our Protestant colleagues saw it quite differently. For her, contemplation was a way of being in the world, a posture with regard to life, a kind of all-inclusive attitude toward oneself, toward others, toward creation, and toward God. Contemplative prayer was not, she believed, a single slice of one's prayer life—time taken out to "do" contemplation—but a totality of outlook, looking at reality the way God looks at it.

The discussion we had around this subject got tense and emotional at several points, because we all had strong opinions on the matter. But we stayed with it and in the end came to agree that our sister was making a valid point, that whatever the "experts" in such matters might say, contemplation needed to be seen in this integrated way—as a way one moves through life. We wound up writing one of our best chapters on Francis and contemplation in that vein, because as we discussed and wrote, it became clear to all of us that Francis's contemplative life happened not only in those well-documented, mystical experiences of ecstatic prayer before the crucifix at the Church of San Damiano or at Mount Alverna when he received the wounds of Christ on his hands and feet. Those were peak moments for sure. But we realized that Francis also walked through the world consciously contemplating God's handprint on everything. His great hymn to Creation, "Blessed are you, my God, for Brother Sun . . . for Sister Moon . . . Sister Water . . . Brother Fire . . . Mother Earth," speaks of an attitude, an awareness, a life fascinated by and wrapped up in a keen sense of God's presence in every speck of creation. His was an ongoing, contemplative response to life.

Whatever the theological merits of our discussion and decision to write about Francis and contemplation that way, it seems clear to me that understanding contemplation as a way of moving through life—trying to see everything in and around us through the eyes of God—is worth thinking about. For one thing, this way of viewing takes the contemplative vocation out of the exclusive domain of cloistered religious like the Trappists and puts it squarely in the nine-to-five, nitty-gritty marketplaces of this world, within the reach of busy, modern people of faith. It invites us to see all reality through the eyes of the Creator and to love the world as God loves it. It also means, I believe, that each of us is called to be a contemplative.

Before continuing with this line of thought and citing examples of contemplatives in the noise and clamor of the world, let me say a word about the traditional cloistered contemplatives. I have no intention whatsoever to imply that the vocation of Trappists or Poor Clares or Carmelites has no place in our hyperactive, goal-oriented society. On the contrary, the men and women who answer the call to spend their lives in the cloister can themselves speak a truly prophetic, corrective word to this empire where "time is money" and where people are judged on how much they have or how much they get done. In that way our contemplative communities do the rest of us an enormous and necessary service, saying with their own lives that the "wasted time" of prayer and silence has a place even and especially in our frenetic culture.

In addition, many of our sisters and brothers who have sensed within themselves a call to the cloistered life find themselves very much in contact with our hurting world. I once led a retreat for a Poor Clare community and found the sisters very much aware and interested in my reflections on engaged spirituality. They kept up with events by reading the newspapers and watching the news on TV, and they showed a lively interest in all sorts of current issues. Naturally, they took all of this to their main work— prayer. Today the Maryknoll Sisters, famous for their activist missioners, maintain cloistered communities in Sudan, Thailand, and Guatemala. That's a telling statement from a group of "doers" about the need for praying with God's word and the newspaper in extremely conflicted areas of the world.

The rural diocese where I served during my years in Bolivia covered a vast area, and our work there with indigenous communities was endless. The bishop of the area took the trouble to invite cloistered sisters into the diocese so that they could learn all about the enormous pastoral challenges we faced and pray for us and with us. Once, during the bishop's absence, I took it on myself to invite a couple of these sisters, who happened to be nurses, on a short mission trip with me. That began a short-lived experience for the nuns, who seemed to appreciate firsthand contact with the extremely poor, marginalized people we were serving. However, the bishop on his return put an immediate stop to the experiment. He insisted that the cloistered religious were there to know about the lives of the people, yes, but above all and exclusively to pray for them. I'm still not sure which of us was right—me with my sort of action-contemplation thrust or the bishop who wanted prayer above all.

A Different Type of Contemplative

In light of the previous story, it's really interesting that one modern icon of cloistered contemplatives, Thomas Merton, had a life-changing—contemplative—epiphany in a totally unexpected

place. Anyone would think that a deeply transformative experience would have happened in the silence of Merton's monastery
at Gethsemani, nestled in the hills of Kentucky, or in the hermit-
age where he lived during the latter part of his life. But as it happened, his breakthrough inspiration took place on a street corner
in the city of Louisville at a moment when he was carrying out
the very ordinary business of going to the doctor. Merton wrote
about the event this way: "On the corner of Fourth and Walnut,
in the center of the shopping district, I was suddenly overwhelmed with the realization that I loved all these people, that
they were mine and I was theirs, that we could not be alien to
one another even though we were total strangers. . . . I have the
immense joy of being human, a member of the race in which God
himself became incarnate."[2] This is a great example of contemplation in the midst of all the noise and bustle of modern life,
which is the point of this reflection on contemplation.

The world today needs people who have this gift of contemplation—and by God's grace we have them, many of them. Some
come immediately to mind, people like Dorothy Day, Archbishop
Oscar Romero, Martin Luther King, Jr., Mahatma Gandhi—
people who lived in modern times, who looked at human situations with the love of the Creator and gave personal testimony to
the way things could be. In the phrases quoted below, note how
these contemplatives deeply appreciated what God has placed in
the human heart and the possibilities each one of them saw
ahead for humanity. And keep in mind that the four people
quoted here led extremely active lives yet still had the capacity to
walk through the world observing everything with the gaze of the
loving Creator.

In 1957, Dorothy Day wrote from the Women's House of
Detention in New York about the privilege of being held there:
"We were, frankly, hoping for jail. Being in jail, one could come
closer to real poverty. Then we would not be running a house of
hospitality, we would not be dispensing food and clothing, we
would not be ministering to the destitute—but we would be truly
one of them."[3]

Archbishop-martyr Oscar Romero of El Salvador had the following to say in the face of threats to his life: "Christ invites us
not to fear persecution because, believe me, brothers and sisters,

we who are committed to the poor must run the same fate as the poor." [4]

Dr. Martin Luther King, Jr., could find a positive (contemplative) side even in the throes of the birthing civil rights movement: "And when we allow freedom ring, when we let it ring from every village and every hamlet, from every state and every city, we will be able to speed up that day when all of God's children, black men and white men, Jews and Gentiles, Protestants and Catholics, will be able to join hands and sing in the words of the old Negro spiritual, 'Free at last, free at last. Thank God Almighty, we are free at last.'" [5]

Mahatma Gandhi could envision the unheard of possibility of forcing the British Empire to leave his beloved India: "These great powers will have to give up their imperialistic ambitions and their exploitation of the so-called semi-civilized nations of the earth and revise their mode of life. It means a complete revolution." [6]

We might not think of these statements as particularly contemplative at first glance. Jail time or civil rights marches or acts of nonviolent resistance don't immediately strike us as the stuff of contemplative prayer. But that is the whole point of looking at contemplation this way. Reading those quotations again, I believe, does open our eyes to loving, Godlike attitudes toward very human and pressing problems—and that for me is a contemplative heart at work. Oscar and Martin, Dorothy and Gandhi were true contemplatives. They looked at reality, especially the great—and small—struggles for human liberation, from God's perspective, seeing possibilities where others might not. They also turned political correctness on its head—another thing real contemplatives do—by celebrating jail time, reveling in being like the poor, overturning racism, and breaking an imperial status quo.

Less widely known people, too, give wonderful examples of what can be done when one has a contemplative attitude. Arthur Simon looked at the scandal of hunger and starvation that millions of people suffer in a world where there is plenty of food and began the organization Bread for the World. Nobel Peace laureate Adolfo Perez-Esquivel saw the human rights abuses taking place in his native Argentina during the "dirty war" there and, at enormous personal risk, initiated a human rights movement to uncover and make public those violations. Sister Dianna Ortiz uses her own dreadful experience of torture as a starting point from which to put in place national and international sanctions against countries—including the United States—that commit these sorts of inhuman, barbaric crimes. If you asked them, Simon, Perez-Esquivel, and Ortiz might laugh at the idea that they are contemplatives in the traditional sense of the word. However, their activities on behalf of a better world, a new humanity if you will, witness to a deeply contemplative spirit in each of them. They go far beyond social activism, anticipating the world that they firmly believe the Creator has in mind for the human family.

Just about everywhere we look there are ordinary people in ordinary situations who view the world the way God does and act on those views. Some time ago an elderly cousin of mine died in a nursing home. During her last months, and especially as she neared death, I could see the staff and assistants of the facility making sure that my cousin kept her dignity despite her almost complete dependence on others. The nurses and aides spoke to her with love and treated her as an adult; when they moved her, they made sure she was comfortable; they cleaned her and fed her with absolute respect. I was so grateful and impressed with these wonderful people, and I felt that their treatment of my dear cousin came from a deep—contemplative—understanding of the inestimable value of each human being.

A young lay missioner I know works in Zambia with children who are dying of AIDS. This has to be the worst kind of experience, to know that these little ones will never grow up and enjoy full lives. I wonder sometimes how she can keep going as she allows her heart to break each time one of them dies. It has to be because she has a contemplative, Godlike understanding of each child's dignity, of God's immense love for these children and of the fact that God is welcoming them home. Otherwise, how could she continue?

A recent immigrant to the United States from Mexico heard about a teen-aged girl in that country who was going blind. The new arrival immediately invited the girl to come here and worked at the thousand and one details of examinations and eventually surgery—complete with financing—so that the girl could have a sighted life. Another example of heroic "orthopraxis" coming out of a contemplative conviction of "what might be."

In the countless struggles for justice and peace and respect for creation there are so many of these contemplatives, people who envision a better way to structure the world, who see the day after tomorrow with all its possibilities in the way I believe God sees it. These modern contemplatives give themselves totally to the "impossible dream."

Right Belief and Right Practice

This way of looking at contemplation runs parallel to a new way of understanding sanctity and holiness. In other times people were considered saintly when they confessed their belief in Jesus in the face of threats, especially when they gave their lives for those beliefs. The Catholic Church celebrates almost every day of the year these confessors and martyrs as great heroes and heroines, which they are. And we've had modern examples of this type of sanctity in places like Nazi concentration camps, behind the Iron Curtain, and in Communist China, where people held on to their faith under terrible pressures to give it up.

But nowadays we're seeing holiness in a new way. People who act on their beliefs, who speak truth to power and put their lives on the line for justice and human dignity, are every bit as heroic—saintly—as the ones who have been officially canonized. It's a shame that the official church has been so slow in recognizing this kind of holiness. Ordinary women and men, however, see it instinctively. Archbishop Romero is already canonized by the Salvadoran people and by so many others who understand that his condemnation of violence, especially by the military in his country, and his assassination at their hands make him the "saint of the Americas."

There are theological words for this shift in emphasis regarding saintliness. Orthodoxy, right belief, used to be the main focus. Now orthopraxis, right action, has taken center stage. I believe the change is healthy and much more in step with the times we live in. The great synodal document *Justice in the World* puts it simply: "Anyone who ventures to speak about justice must first be just in their eyes" (no. 40). People today accept nothing less.

"Social" Contemplation

As we moved through the decade of the 1990s and approached the new millennium, people all over the world recalled the Jubilee ideal of "restoring right relationships" embedded in the Jewish and Christian traditions and began applying it to the world debt. At first, the idea of reducing or eliminating the suffocating payments owed by debtor countries to international lending organizations or to banks in the developed world seemed like a pipe dream. But these contemplatives continued to analyze the issue, outline practical steps to achieve their goal, and press for dialogues with the lending institutions. They got the attention of people in organizations like the World Bank and the International Monetary Fund, and some progress was made. Despite the fact that their dream of eliminating world debt as a new millennium dawned came up short, still an ideal was planted in the hearts of millions around the world—one that some day will surely be realized. All because a few "ordinary" contemplatives looked at a complicated, nearly intractable problem with fresh eyes—with God's eyes. Theirs was a vision as bold as Gandhi's when he calmly told the British Empire that they would have to leave India.

An interesting anecdote says a great deal about the impact these "dreamers" have on the bureaucrats who serve international lending institutions. Marie Dennis, one of the leaders in debt-relief efforts, has dialogued frequently with the "experts" inside the walls of the World Bank and International Monetary Fund. They know Marie to be serious, well-prepared, and respectful of them in these conversations, and she has won their respect. One Good Friday dozens of people engaged in a Way of the Cross that included a stop at the World Bank, one symbol of why Jesus' suffering continues in the world. To dramatize our reason for being in that place, Marie and several others sat in the doorway of the building in an act of civil disobedience. When the World Bank employees heard that Marie Dennis might be arrested there, they were horrified. Word came down from the corporate offices inviting Marie and others to come upstairs and dialogue. Her reply: "There are days for dialogue and there are

days for direct action; today [Good Friday] is a day for action."
Again, a Gandhian (contemplative) view of things.

The French philosopher Albert Camus once stated that the
world will only be saved through beauty. His insight underscores,
I believe, the contemplative capacity in each of our hearts. To
appreciate beauty and try to create it especially in the midst of
the ugliness that threatens every dimension of human life, I believe, is the outlook and the purpose of people who see the shape
of our world as God sees it. We're not speaking here of the usual
ideas of beauty—lovely art or inspired music. We mean the
beauty of a human person who was dead because of physical,
mental, or social deprivations and now lives because those oppressions have been lifted; the beauty of a child born into poverty,
who because of some miracle is flourishing. To see beauty in this
way is the result of prayer and a contemplative way of being fully
alive and observant in this world. While there will always be a
need for "solid moments before the Lord," getting away from the
intensity of daily life and becoming lost in prayer, and while the
vocation to a cloistered life will continue to grace the church, numberless ordinary men and women of faith keep hearing God's call
to move through life, seeing it and loving it as the Creator does,
celebrating beauty and promoting it—contemplatives all.

Contemplatives also see the tragedy of beauty that gets snuffed
out and of ugliness that permeates the lives and surroundings of
too many human beings. Our country's policies bear much of the
responsibility for these wrongs. It's sufficient just to mention
places like Iraq and Afghanistan, issues like free-trade agreements
and weapons sales, situations like global warming and air pollution to see what the contemplatives see in our national life.
That's the reason so many of them engage in public protests, or,
like Marie Dennis, denounce these policies through dialogue *and*
civil disobedience, or who walk the halls of Congress in an effort
to change our country's direction.

Conclusion

A final story reemphasizes this reflection on engaged, worldly
prayer and contemplation, and brings it to a conclusion. One of

the brightest and most faith-filled persons I ever knew was a husband, father, and lawyer who for more than half of his adult life was politically engaged in this country's national politics, always looking for ways to improve life for the neediest. Later in life he taught law at a prestigious university, hoping to pass on his passion to younger generations. At about age sixty my friend was diagnosed with terminal cancer and gradually declined to the point where he became entirely bedridden. I visited him not long before he died, and he told me that he continued to read the morning paper "so that I know what to pray for each day." To the end of his life my friend's prayer was worldly, "distracted" and done, literally, with the newspaper and the Bible in his hands—and this prayer was surely contemplative.

Chapter 4

• • • • •

Sin and Grace

During the first days of the brutal 1973 military takeover in Chile, thousands of ordinary citizens were rounded up and held as real or perceived threats to the new regime of General Augusto Pinochet. One of those arrested that day was a popular young composer and singer named Victor Jara, whose music often poked fun at upper-class pretensions and the glaring inequalities in the country. He had been doing a concert at the Catholic University of Santiago on the morning of the coup and was taken to the national football (soccer) stadium, which had become a makeshift prison due to the overwhelming number of people arrested by the military.

Victor's British-born wife later told the rest of the tragic story. She searched for her husband during those awful days following the military crackdown and finally received an anonymous phone call telling her that she could pick up Victor's body at the city morgue. There she found out that he had been summarily executed a day or two after his arrest; she also saw that his hands were mutilated. Later, people who had survived the detention at the stadium came to tell her that in the first hours there Victor was leading songs in an effort to keep up everyone's spirits and that the soldiers broke his hands to prevent him from playing his guitar. Afterward, they killed him.

I choose that sad story as an entry point for this chapter on the sin and evil that shroud our world and on their polar opposite—grace and goodness. It was sheer evil that brought about the torture and death of Victor Jara; but in the short time between his arrest and death I believe that Victor proved to be a grace for his companions in that football stadium. Sin and grace are realities that have to be factored into an engaged Christian spirituality, because otherwise we run the risk of ignoring another essential aspect of life in God—in this case the timeless struggle between evil and good at every level of our human existence. It is said that many people have lost a sense of sin. People talk about dysfunctional families, or childhood traumas, or addictions for which we are not responsible as explanations for wrongful behavior. Victor Jara's story, I think, brings the realness of sin crashing back into our consciousness. There is no getting around the naked evil that was done to him. For those who try to live faithfully in the heart of this empire, that realization is absolutely crucial.

Personal Sin and Interpersonal Considerations

In mainstream Catholic-Christian spirituality our understanding of personal sin has deepened and matured in the decades since the Second Vatican Council. Thank God we no longer hold a magnifying glass over each of our actions and make those tortured examinations of conscience we once did to figure out if we have somehow fallen into sin over the previous hours or days. (Vowed religious used to perform both a general examination and what was called a particular examen regarding some specific fault they were trying to overcome.) Happily, that sort of scrupulous attention to each of our daily activities has given way to a much healthier, but I think no less responsible, questioning of our fundamental option—where our life is moving in general terms. Far from denying sin in our lives, this way of looking at our life helps us to take stock of our overall direction and possible obstacles— sins—that can cause detours on our journey toward God.

Furthermore, in the past years we have become more aware that the relational/interpersonal aspects of life also play an important role in examining our fundamental option. This is sort of new for us after so many years of thinking about sin as a private matter between "me and God." We give special attention these days to how we treat others, how we use or misuse any power or influence we have in people's lives, and especially, how we act in behalf of the poor and needy. It was long past time for this corrective, because one of Jesus' central teachings is exactly about how we treat the "other," especially the "other" who is in trouble. This is the best barometer for judging our relationship with God. "Those who say, 'I love God,' and hate their brothers or sisters, are liars" (1 Jn 4:20). The way we handle our human relationships is an accurate measure of how we are with God and where we find ourselves along a spectrum that runs from one of the big sins of our culture, self-absorption, to that rare commodity, selflessness.

Social Sin

The personal and interpersonal aspects of morality have gotten all sorts of attention in Catholic-Christian spirituality. Here I want to spend more time on a dimension that has not, one that the bishops of Latin America pointed out in 1968. When they wrote in the Medellín document *Justice and Peace* that the basically unjust Latin-American social structures that trapped the majority of people there in varying degrees of dehumanized poverty, they described it as "institutionalized violence" (no. 16). They meant that violence and sin are embedded in the very fabric of the society—in the economic, political, racial, sociological, and yes, religious realities that affect the lives of all peoples living on that continent—both the poor and the wealthy. When I first heard the words *institutionalized violence*, it was like a curtain being pulled back and a whole new reality opening for me. In an instant my understanding of sin expanded to include all those things in a society or culture that cut off human beings from a full life—things like malnutrition, illiteracy, unemployment, racism, classism, sexism, and so on. Institutional violence also includes all those things that help the privileged "advance on the backs of the poor." This is *social sin*. I believe that being conscious of the presence of social sin in the world is essential for anyone who wants to cultivate a valid spirituality today, particularly in the United States.

Still, a lot of people find it hard to understand the social dimension of sin—or they don't want to. It's common to hear, for example, that the sins of society are simply the result of each person's failings and that if we bring about the conversion of every individual, society's problems will disappear. This is one of those half-truths that cause more confusion. Naturally, if everyone were converted, say, to gospel living, society would be far better off. But the sins of our times go way beyond individual responsibility. Hunger, racism, poverty—just to name three—are evils that have become embedded in the way our world is organized. They are not one person's responsibility. But they do stand under a much-needed gospel judgment, just as much as do individual and interpersonal sins.

To press this all-important point: if sin is reduced solely to personal failings, where would we place the responsibility for the torture and death of Victor Jara? With the soldiers who mutilated his hands and later executed him? With their immediate military superiors, without whose explicit or implicit orders the ordinary soldiers would never have done what they did? Or do we hold responsible the leaders of the regime that seized power in Chile on September 11, 1973, and, in one way or another, did away with anyone who opposed them? Or perhaps we should lay Jara's torture and death at the feet of individuals in the United States government who fostered and supported the military overthrow. But no, we really cannot pinpoint personal guilt here, even if we'd like to. All of those just mentioned participated in this crime. All were guilty, yet no one was immediately responsible. It was an institutional sin. What is clear is that a socially sinful establishment took over in Chile that day—backed by the United States—and Victor Jara's case, like the thousands in the years that followed, is a dreadful example of what results from institutionalized evil. This is an important concept to grasp.

A few years ago a friend of mine in the U.S. State Department asked me to give a conference to a large group of high-ranking military officers from several countries in Latin America. They were studying at a center in Washington DC run by the U.S. government, which prepares people like these for high positions in their country's national military and political establishments. The topic assigned to me had something to do with moral aspects of social change in Latin America, and the officers offered no particular objections to what I had to say concerning better distribution of resources among their people, education for all sectors of their societies, or even my thoughts about the obscene expenditures on the military and on armaments in their countries. However, when I began to talk about institutionalized violence in their countries, the reaction was immediate. They challenged the notion that evil and injustice reside in the social constructs of every country. The question-and-answer period became quite heated and spilled over into our coffee break. I wondered if their upset with me on this point stemmed from a religious fundamentalism that I thought I noticed in how they came at the question—or was it perhaps defensiveness about the military (sinful?) structures these men obviously represented?

Finally, I decided to diffuse the emotion around the question of social sin by using a clear example of it from U.S. history. I asked them where they would put the responsibility for the institution of slavery that marred the first eighty years of our national life. With the bounty hunters who tracked down Africans and hauled them in chains to our shores? With the slave owners in this country who bought and sold black people as property? With individual lawmakers who voted time after time for legal protection of this unbelievably unjust social system? Or perhaps with our revered Founding Fathers, who crafted a Bill of Rights that was actually based on the premise of "liberty and justice— *for [some, but not] all*"? I tried to point out that slavery is a social evil. That long chapter in U.S. history proved that no amount of personal conversion was able to overcome it. In the end it required a social upheaval, the bloody Civil War fought in this country, as well as continued action by our government at every level to carry out the great unfinished business we still have in our society: "liberty and justice *for all*." By using this example from U.S. history, I think I made some headway with my audience that day. In any case, the institution of slavery in the United States is for me a compelling, here-at-home demonstration of institutionalized social sin.

Once a person has come to understand the concept of institutionalized sin, it is easy to point out any number of examples. I've already mentioned racism, world hunger, and poverty. We can also name the death penalty, abortion, ecological destruction, classism, militarism, consumerism—the list is long. And for each of these sins the same questions arise: Who is at fault here? Who bears the ultimate responsibility? And always the answer comes back: no one, and everyone because these are sins that have become institutionalized.

As U.S. Americans I believe it's enormously important to think about social sin in the light of our country's projections across the world. We are the only superpower today, and what we do and don't do affect just about every part of the globe. The recent history of Nicaragua, El Salvador, and Guatemala—and U.S. interference in those countries—provides case studies in this regard. In Nicaragua our government decided that the Sandinista revolution had a Marxist-Leninist color to it, so we took it upon ourselves to start a counter-revolution and install "our" type of government there. El Salvador suffered for more than a decade from a civil war, fomented by the United States, even after the archbishop of that country pleaded publicly with American President Jimmy Carter not to send more weapons to the Salvadoran military. Our direct overthrow in 1954 of a democratically elected president in Guatemala led to forty years of military repression and hundreds of thousands of deaths there. We continue our lethal meddling today, most notably in places like Iraq, Iran, and Afghanistan. All of these national actions are institutionalized evils, committed by the United States of America. They call for an examination of conscience by people of faith here. This must become a part of our personal and collective spirituality.

Personal Guilt in Social Sin

Institutionalized sin inevitably makes us ask about each individual's responsibility. I've tried to insist here that none of these social evils is our personal fault, though at times individuals can surely be directly implicated in them. However, we in the First World do participate in them, sometimes as victims but more often as beneficiaries in this affluent world of ours. On a planet divided between the "haves" and the "have nots," between those who have too much to eat and those who starve, between almost limitless opportunity and snuffed out hopes—we in the First World should be conscious of where we stand. We are the

rich man of Jesus' parable about Lazarus, dressing well and din-
ing sumptuously every day.

It's important for us to keep this fact in mind if we are to live
an honest, gospel spirituality. We cannot close our eyes to these
global realities. I am not trying to paralyze anyone with guilt, as
I hope will be clear below. But I do believe it's necessary to admit the fact that structural evil, while not our personal responsibility, very often works in favor of those of us who live in the
developed, privileged, affluent world and, at the same time,
works against our brothers and sisters in the underdeveloped,
underprivileged, impoverished world. Examples of this are all
around us.

Some years ago a Franciscan brother of mine returned to the
United States after years as a missionary in a poor country.
Shortly before he left there, a woman asked him to let her know
if what she had heard could be remotely possible: that in the
United States people take showers and flush their toilets with
pure, drinkable water.

The June 7, 2004, issue of *Time Magazine* ran a cover story on
the increasing number of obese persons in the United States. The
statistics on this problem are startling, especially when set alongside the numbers of hungry people in the world. *Time* reported,
quoting figures from the Center for Disease Control, that fully
two-thirds of the 300 million Americans are overweight, and almost one-third of us are obese. A United Nations agency has
found that 828 million people in the world (nearly one-sixth of
the human race) suffer from starvation. This divide in our world
is much more complicated when we factor in the obesity of all
those people who are too poor to afford a balanced diet and eat
only cheap, starchy foods.

Much closer to home, a couple of years ago I began to have
chest pains during exercise. A visit to my cardiologist and some
sophisticated tests showed a significant blockage in one of my
main coronary arteries. In a matter of days a stent was put into
the affected artery by a team of highly skilled cardiac surgeons,
nurses, and technicians, and my problem was solved, at least for
the time being. The procedure and an overnight stay in the hospital, "just as a precaution," cost $11,000, which my insurance
carrier paid in full. All that effort and expense just to give this

seventy year old a reprieve from his progressive coronary-artery disease in a world where most babies die before they reach five years of age, where young people often die of a burst appendix, and where pregnant women lose their babies because there are no midwives!

Acknowledging that these global inequities are tilted in favor of us in the developed world is an act of honesty and, I think, repentance. It's essential for genuine life in God, and it puts me in mind of Francis of Assisi when he called himself "the worst of all sinners." I could never figure out how someone like that, who was so clearly a moral person, could say such a thing about himself until I came to understand social sin. Then I thought that perhaps this son of a prosperous cloth merchant saw his privileged life in relation to the impoverishment of others. Maybe Francis understood in those very early days of capitalism that his family's class was getting rich at the expense of others. And maybe it was for that reason that his conversion to God came through a conscious identification with those same poor brothers and sisters.

At the same time, it would be wrong for anyone to become paralyzed with guilt over the fact that our advantages so often result from enormous disadvantages worldwide. God doesn't love us because we are sinless but rather despite our sins. What this insane global arrangement ought to do is push us to act in behalf of poor people, even at the cost of diminishment in our own privileged status. As a matter of fact, I know a great number of people in solidarity movements with underdeveloped countries and needy people whose motivation comes right out of this honest awareness of their privilege in a mostly underprivileged world. They are the best of the best, because they have turned their own comfort and affluence into service. As their consciousness of being a part of the social sin that afflicts so many in our world gets clearer, they hold firmly to the truth that they are loved sinners. In my own life this awareness of God's immense mercy toward us who live well at the expense of others has been a freeing experience and one that serves as a powerful motivation to do what I can to overcome the terrible injustices in our world. Knowing our privileged place in this world and the underprivilege of vast numbers of our sisters and brothers helps us to make our own the prayer, "Lord, be merciful to me a sinner"—and then go do something about the sin.

Finally, when we look at ourselves as citizens of the United States, everything we've said about living well at the expense of others becomes all the more relevant. That's really the whole point of this section on institutionalized sin—societies, political structures, national and international arrangements almost always favor some over others. This is true inside and outside of our country, with its immense power and influence, where the rich get richer and the poor get left behind. It's ironic that the United States will do anything to keep this imbalance in place. We've been told by our government, for example, that our military adventurism in the Middle East is justified "to protect our way of life." So our sense of needing God's mercy stretches out to include especially our country and all of us who live here. I think here about the part of the eucharistic liturgy when the community takes a moment to ask for God's mercy "for what we have done and what we have failed to do." It would be good for presiders and other leaders of prayer to include in those acts of repentance and reconciliation some indication that we are doing them in the name of our country as well as in our own names. Maybe some day the formula for those acts of contrition will say: "I confess . . . what I have done and what I have failed to do, what our country has done and what it has failed to do."

That entire reflection on sin, especially its social aspects and our role in them, takes us seamlessly and immediately to the polar opposite of evil—grace. It is important for us to look at grace so we don't get fixated on sin. The Catholic-Christian view of things holds that grace, not sin, has the final word: humanity and the world are not condemned to fail; the light will prevail; goodness will overcome. God's light and life shine on in human beings and in the world.

Grace

It's helpful, I think, to look at grace in the light of the same three dimensions of life emphasized in this book—the personal, the interpersonal and the social. Individually, each one of us senses the power of grace in our personal journey through life. We all feel those daily, ordinary inspirations to do the kind action, to avoid a hurtful word, to live with integrity. These graces come to us in thousands of daily situations. Sometimes we accept them, and sometimes we don't. But they keep coming, and we can thank God for them, hoping we don't neglect them too often.

We've all experienced special personal graces when we've had to make important decisions or when particularly difficult or challenging situations faced us, haven't we? Once I was offered the job as justice and peace director for a mid-sized diocese in the United States. I first thought that it would be a good fit for me. I liked the people who were working in the same field, and my interview for the job went quite well. But in the end I decided not to accept the position. At the last minute something told me that I wouldn't be the right person for it. Later, with that clarity which comes from hindsight, I saw what a mistake it would have been for me to take the job. Basically, that justice and peace office did urban U.S. ministry, and my whole experience up to that time was international. I know it was a real grace that steered me away from work for which I really had no preparation.

The story of Salvadoran Archbishop Oscar Romero's conversion, and the part that Jesuit Rutilio Grande played in it, is a great example of personal grace at work. In March 1977, the conservative, traditional Romero had just taken on his responsibilities as head of San Salvador's archdiocese, to the delight of many repressive forces in that country. They saw him as an ally in keeping the progressive wing of the church in check. Then Romero's friend, Father Grande was gunned down because he was defending his oppressed parishioners. It was a *kairos* (timely and holy, grace-filled) moment for the archbishop, and he was never the same again. He immediately took up the prophetic mantle Rutilio had left behind and became a powerful spokesman for the disenfranchised of El Salvador. Almost exactly three years later, in March 1980, Archbishop Romero followed Father Grande in martyrdom, an example of grace building on grace.

That wonderful story highlights a second dimension of life, good relationships and what a grace they are. Oscar Romero and Rutilio Grande had become friends during the time that they lived in a seminary community some years before. Romero admired

Grande as a man of prayer and a good pastor. When Rutilio was killed, Romero saw that those very qualities were seen as threats to the brutal status quo of El Salvador at that time, and from that day on he imitated the example of his martyred friend. God gives us friendship, love, and intimacy to encourage and console and empower us. We all know examples of these interpersonal graces, and any one of us, I'm sure, could relate dozens of instances when we became more than we could ever have believed possible thanks to the encouragement of a loved one, a mentor, a teacher.

I remember vividly as a sophomore in college walking across campus one fall evening with a group of classmates on the way to a movie. We stopped to chat with a young faculty member, one of the many Franciscans who ran the university. For some reason the priest singled me out to ask: "Why don't you put on the brown?" [the color of the Franciscan garb]. I couldn't get his question out of my mind, and two weeks later I was knocking on his door to talk with him about it. (The friar told me that he had no memory of saying any such thing to me.) As it turned out that "throw-away" question of his began a wonderful lifelong friendship between us and sparked my journey as a member of the Order of St. Francis.

In our inner-city community we have a young man who teaches in a middle school for at-risk boys. He also doubles as their soccer coach. Recently, their team won a city-wide championship, beating better-equipped suburban boys. It was a great victory for the underdogs, but our community member most celebrated the values of teamwork and sportsmanship his boys showed on the field—the same values he tries to instill each day in the classroom. There is no doubt that his teen-agers will remember this father-figure and mentor and what he taught them for the rest of their lives. Grace at work in interpersonal relations.

This sort of grace also helps us avoid the kinds of relationships that are off limits, out of bounds. A priest friend of mine recently told me that he once had to ask to be transferred from a ministry he loved and one where he was doing very useful work. He had become very much attracted to a married woman who was working with him, and it was clear that staying where he was could do a lot of harm to the woman and her husband, to the priest himself, and to the ministry. So he moved. Grace prevailed. If more priests, religious, and bishops had taken those kinds of grace-inspired decisions, we wouldn't be in the middle of a disastrous clergy scandal today.

Grace as a Social Reality

When we think about them, we have no trouble recognizing these personal and interpersonal inspirations as graces. They are all around us. We know that they come from God. It seems to me that what we now have to get our heads around is grace as a social reality—institutionalized grace. In a world, especially our U.S. world, where there is enormous structural sin, it's important to recognize that grace works on those evils as well. There are many examples of God's life permeating and pushing back the darkness and evil in the fabric of societies and replacing them with good laws and policies and efforts to make human life better. In fact, I believe that for every single social sin we can name there is a corresponding social grace given by God to combat the evil. Some examples:

The Peace Movement

The worldwide peace movement, which has grown stronger and more articulate over the last decades, is a good example of this type of grace. In the last half-century humanity has moved from a kind of resigned acceptance that war is pretty much inevitable in the affairs of countries and peoples to a growing conviction that war is futile and never really solves conflicts among peoples. We had a great example of this new consciousness playing out as our country's leaders moved toward what they euphemistically called "regime change" in Iraq. Literally millions of people took to the streets across the world to insist that America was making a huge mistake. In the face of U.S. aggression against Iraq, Pope John Paul II put all of this opposition into a single phrase: "War is always a defeat for humanity." Now, several years later, it's tragically clear how right that opposition was. Resistance to war is a new consciousness—a new social grace.

What is more, the traditional just-war theory, the conditions that academics and theologians set out for a war to be considered morally permissible, is more and more being rejected. People have come to understand that there probably never was a way to justify such horrendous and dangerous "solutions" to national and international disputes—and there surely is none at this time in history. There are many reasons for this sea change in humanity's perception of war—in particular the frightening power of nuclear weapons. Another powerful reason, I believe, is the consistent efforts of peace groups to point out the absolute uselessness of military solutions. The whole world is aware now of the analyses, prayers, and public actions of peace people worldwide in the last decades—including and especially dramatic antiwar gestures that often bring with them long stays in jail. This long-term work stands as a great example of social grace.

Secular Grace

World hunger, dehumanizing poverty, racism, sexism, disregard for life in all its forms and at every stage, environmental degradation, consumerism, materialism, militarism, torture—all the social sins we can possibly list—have movements of good people working to overcome them. We know that a lot of these efforts come out of simple good will, wanting to do the right thing, and not because of any particular faith perspective or religious motivation. But they are graces nevertheless. Jesus said it best. When the disciples wanted to stop someone who was doing good works "because he is not of our company," Jesus said, "Do not stop him, for any man who is not against you is on your side" (Lk 9:49–50). If we are honest with ourselves, we have to admit that some of the best work being done in the world today doesn't rely on any kind of spirituality. It's good-willed people responding to needs they see. Those of us who do claim a particular religious tradition—particularly, a Christian spirituality—have a lot to think about here. Where is grace working best, and among whom?

The much-criticized and maligned (by the United States) United Nations exemplifies just this sort of nonreligious but authentic grace in our world. In fact, the concept of a secular world

forum where nation-states and all sorts of lesser bodies can dis-
cuss their issues on something of an equal footing and try to resolve their conflicts has been affirmed and celebrated consistently
in Catholic social teaching.

In 1941, four years before the establishment of the United
Nations, Pope Pius XII in his Christmas message called for an
"international order, which, while assuring a just and lasting
peace to all peoples, will bring forth well-being and prosperity"
(no. 17). Blessed John XXIII wrote in *Pacem in Terris* in 1963: "It
is our earnest prayer that the United Nations—in its structure
and its means—may become ever more equal to the magnitude
and nobility of its tasks" (no. 145). And the great 1971 Synod of
Bishops proclaimed in *Justice in the World*: "Let the United Nations—which because of its unique purpose should promote participation by all nations—and international organizations be supported" (no. 65).

These are stirring words from the Catholic tradition about an
organization that has no explicit connection with faith or religion. They surely mean that the church understands grace in the
broadest way—anything which promotes the well-being of
peoples, especially of the neediest. To put it another way, Catholic social teaching sees as graces any and all efforts to build a
world more in keeping with God's reign on earth. So, let me say
it once again: to be authentic, Catholic-Christian spirituality has
to take this perception of God's action in history seriously into
consideration, whether or not that action is connected with explicit religiosity. "Any man who is not against you is on your
side." Maybe the bigger question for people of faith is, Are we on
the side of those who are doing God's work today?

That brings up serious questions for U.S. Catholic-Christians.
Where do we come down on the policies of our country? Do we
judge them in the light of God's liberating action in history—or
do we have a sort of knee-jerk attitude that the United States is
right no matter what it does and that it's unpatriotic to criticize
our country? Let me give an example of what I mean. Right after the overthrow of the Somoza dictatorship in Nicaragua, some
U.S. missioners there invited me to come and see what was going on. One of the meetings I had was with a middle-class Nica-
raguan Catholic whose comments I never forgot. He said that

after the fighting stopped, Cuba sent doctors and teachers to help repair and rebuild his country. The United States, on the other hand, began sending weapons to undermine the new government. The man's question was this: who are our real friends? The deeper question, I believe, is this one: who really was doing God's work there—Cuba or the United States? I think that all of us in this country have to ask where our loyalty lies—with those who are trying to do good in the world, or with an unquestioning "patriotism." Where is grace at work?

Ecological Peace

We're gradually coming to see that the planet earth, our fragile home in a vast universe, has been suffering because of institutionalized sin. So all of the efforts to signal the dangers to our environment and to repair it are graces. Chapter 8 is devoted to ecology as a modern and vital part of Catholic-Christian spirituality. Let me just say here that the growing concern for the earth, our mother and life source, and the increasing number of movements to save our planet represent God-given grace at work on a sin that threatens the environment that holds the very future of humanity.

The Sacrament of Reconciliation

One great grace that the Catholic-Christian tradition has received to overcome evil is that special encounter with Christ we call the sacrament of reconciliation. It points to and makes real God's unbelievable mercy toward us and our world, no matter how horrendous the sin. I've come to believe that celebrating this sacrament, individually or communally, is another powerful way of pushing back the evil in our lives and in the world in order to replace it with grace.

Since the Second Vatican Council the numbers of people celebrating this sacrament have dramatically decreased. Perhaps this is because we saw that the old confession of sins had become trivialized—a routine listing of meaningless faults like "I missed my morning prayers," or "I lost my temper." Or maybe it was that other expressions of sorrow for sin, such as the communal Penitential Rite at the beginning of Mass, made much more sense to us. It might have been, too, that in the euphoria of the Second Vatican Council and its great themes of salvation history and God's overwhelming love for everything human, the sense of personal and social sin took a back seat in our consciousness.

But sin is still very much with us. So it's clear that an authentic Catholic-Christian spirituality has to include a keen awareness both of evil and of the need for repentance. The opportunity to ritualize that awareness in the sacrament of reconciliation is appropriate and necessary, particularly for those of us who live in the United States. Just like each of the other sacraments, in which we touch the Divine at peak moments (birth, entering adulthood, needing food for life's journey, entering a lifelong covenanted relationship, engaging in priestly service, and dying), the sacrament of reconciliation helps us to reach out to a forgiving Christ as flawed people in a flawed world.

To take this a little further, after coming to understand institutionalized sin, I've always felt that confession ought to include not only personal faults and failings but also the divisions, hurts, injustices, deprivations, and exclusions that we see all around us. Yet, after more than four decades of priestly ministry, I can remember only one occasion when a person confessed a social sin. It had to do with her job in a large corporation whose policies she believed were unethical. We need a lot more education in this regard.

Furthermore, we U.S. Americans stand before God in the sacrament of reconciliation as citizens of a country that does good in the world, yes, but immense harm as well; a land that has been graced with plenty, but in which even millions of its own people are deprived; a superpower that has become an enormous burden on the rest of the world. So we have to mediate, repent, and reconcile as members of Christ's body in the United States today. Jesus did exactly that on the cross—"it was our infirmities he bore" (Is 53:4). We do it in his place now. There's a whole spirituality of reparation and reconciliation that comes out of this reflection.

Penitence

One crucial and ongoing mindset that we Catholic-Christian people in the United States ought to have is penitence. The model for us, I think, is the story of Jonah in the Hebrew scriptures. He very reluctantly took a call from God to "set out for the great city of Nineveh and preach against it," calling its entire population to a change of heart. Our country is in dire need of conversion, the kind that even the king of Nineveh accepted: "The people of Nineveh . . . proclaimed a fast and all of them, great and small, put on sackcloth. . . . The king rose from his throne, laid aside his robe, covered himself with sackcloth and sat in the ashes" (Jon 3:5–6).

As a citizen of the U.S. empire, I've been fascinated with this story of Jonah, which we hear every year at the beginning of Lent. I believe it applies directly to us and dream of a moment when all of us, from the president to the smallest child, will "cover ourselves with sackcloth and sit in ashes." But I'd suggest that, for us, the change of heart that Jonah called for doesn't really have to do with sackcloth and ashes but with cutting back on our conspicuous consumption of resources, walking gently on the earth, respecting life, allowing people to be different. Living at the center of what Pope John Paul II called a culture of death, we need to stand against the death of having too much stuff, of waste, of capital punishment, of preemptive war, of sexual excess and exploitation, of fearing to speak out.

There are obvious acts of penitence that would both serve as correctives and speak loudly to our culture that has lost its way. Eating moderately, turning off the blaring television and radio sets, ignoring the rampant exploitation of the female body, using resources like electricity and water sparingly, reading worthwhile material, making room for silence in one's life, prayerfully reflecting on the priorities our faith inspires in contradistinction to those held out to us by our government and the advertising and entertainment industries—all of these practices would mark us as Christians who happen to be U.S. Americans, not U.S. Americans who happen to be Christians. They would also keep our minds sharp and our hearts supple as we move into the public arenas of this country to effect justice and equity.

These are not popular or even widely accepted thoughts, precisely because of what we're told about being patriotic and because of the deadly self-absorption which the empire assures us will make us happy. But I'm convinced that our society is in more danger of destruction than Nineveh was, and only the kind of total conversion that happened there can save us.

Conclusion

These are heavy thoughts. But then sin and grace are heavy topics. So perhaps a story of grace overcoming sin will bring this chapter to a positive close and put an exclamation point on it. The story begins in the darkness of sin; it ends in the light of grace.

On a November night in 1989, a squad of Salvadoran military personnel forced its way into the Jesuit residence at the University of Central America and brutally murdered six priests and two of their lay associates. The army had decided that they were a threat to the status quo and had to be eliminated.

That crime was clearly an awful example of evil at work and underscores the main point of this chapter: the struggle between the power of sin and the power of good continues. The Jesuits and their co-workers were trying to bring about peace in an environment of war; the military that killed them wanted no part of that peace. This particular story doesn't end there, however, but continues and demonstrates how grace can overcome even the worst sin.

A seventh member of the Jesuit community that was brutalized that November night, theologian Jon Sobrino, was traveling in Asia at that time and escaped the fate of the others. His hurried trip back to El Salvador a few days after the tragedy took him through Washington DC, where he met with several of us who knew him. We fully expected to encounter a broken man, someone who had just lost lifelong friends, brother Jesuits, colleagues in the outstanding educational center that they had built up. What would our conversation be like? Would there be anything we could say to mitigate the enormous pain Father Sobrino had to be experiencing?

What we found was a person obviously in deep mourning, who grasped fully the immensity of what had happened to his brothers and co-workers. But that day Father Sobrino also exhibited amazing serenity and spoke of his belief that life outlasts death. I remember watching him closely as he spoke of his absolute conviction that "death does not have the final word—life does." There was not the slightest indication that this priest, theologian, and teacher was telling us what he felt we needed to hear; on the contrary, it was clear to me that those Easter words came from the depths of his Christian soul.

To experience Father Sobrino's living testimony to the resurrection at a moment when everything within him must have been pulling in the direction of despair convinced us that here was a man of deep spirituality, sorrowful yes, but alive and hope-filled in a world that had crashed into chaos around him. He was grace in the face of sin.

As a matter of fact, the brutal slayings at the University of Central America so shocked El Salvador and the world that a lagging peace process in that country took on new vigor. Within a relatively short time after the massacre the opposing factions—a popular insurgency and a U.S.-backed military establishment—sat down together and did precisely what the martyred Jesuits had been promoting. They negotiated what turned out to be a lasting peace accord and finally brought an end to eleven years of civil war in that country. As Jon Sobrino predicted, life did eventually have the final word.

The conviction expressed by Father Sobrino that day is in the final analysis a concrete, real-life example of God's greatest gift to humanity—hope in the midst of sin and suffering and tragedy. Death is not the last chapter. It does not have the final say. Life does. We have God's word for it: "the light shines on in the darkness, a darkness that did not overcome it" (Jn 1:5); "where sin increased, grace abounded all the more" (Rom 5:21). Belief in life conquering death, goodness overcoming evil, grace overpowering sin, is hope—the all-important theological virtue that several writers have called the future tense of faith. Hope, the Easter virtue, is the Christian's contribution; it is the only unique element we can bring to all the efforts good-willed people make to do the right thing in this world and to help goodness triumph.

It seems to me that our post-9/11 United States needs a large dose of hope. The vicious attacks on our country and so many innocent people that September day have traumatized us more, perhaps, than we can yet calculate. Unfortunately, however, the leaders of this nation decided to play off of that trauma and use fear to set an agenda of aggression. So now we have the quagmires of Afghanistan and Iraq and only God knows what awaits us. I believe that we who pledge allegiance to the One who rose from the dead have a historic opportunity and obligation to speak and live a word of hope today in our country. Because beyond all of the code reds, the security measures, and the dire warnings that are thrown at us, one truth spoken by Jesus stands out: "Fear is useless" (Mk 5:36).

Grace will not be denied by sin.

Chapter 5

• • • • •

Obedience

Two connected events in my life come to mind as a starting point for these thoughts on obedience. One happened during my

---

Chapters 5 and 6 take up obedience, poverty, and chastity. While we usually think of them as the public vows made by people called to religious life, I want to emphasize that all Catholic-Christian spirituality includes these values. I believe we are all called to obey God, stand with the poor, and live with integrity in our relationships, whether or not we've made vows.

At the same time, I'm convinced that vowing obedience, poverty and chastity in religious life has a social dimension. It is a much-needed prophetic stand in the midst of a culture that too often dismisses obedience to anything except our own individual fulfillment, ignores the poor, and scoffs at self-restraint in sexual matters.

Sister Barbara O'Dea, superior general of her religious congregation, the Daughters of Wisdom, spoke about the social implications of the vows in a Lenten message to her sisters some years ago. "For today's world the language of the Cross is indeed folly. Only faith and Wisdom can reveal the Cross-Resurrection as inseparable. Evil is so tangible. We see it in the limitless accumulation of wealth by the few and the ever-increasing misery of so many millions of people. It reveals itself in abuse of power by the few and the oppression, even slaughter of so many. Its seductive rhetoric of sexual liberation masks new forms of slavery and even slave trade. As I ponder these evils, it strikes me that there is tremendous unexplored potential in the witness of our vows *lived radically*" (*Sagesse Internationale* 24 [March 1998], emphasis added).

Chapters 5 and 6 are attempts at the exploration that Sister Barbara called for.

first overseas assignment in Bolivia. I was well into my fourth year of what I felt was a fairly useful and certainly a fulfilling ministry in that country, when out of the blue I received word from my Franciscan superior in New York that I was forthwith assigned to Lima, Peru. The news took me completely by surprise. No consultation had preceded it; no warning had been given. Just a one-line telegram (in those days before email) telling me to pack up and go, and that instructions would follow. So, I went. That was the understanding we all had of the vow of obedience in those days. You did what you were told by your superiors. Later I found out that I was being sent to begin a new parish in a suburb of Lima.[1]

The connected event happened several years later when another superior of my Franciscan province visited me at the parish in Lima, which by that time had developed into quite a unique and challenging ministry. As the time for the visit approached, I knew that I had some thoughts of my own about where I could best minister after finishing my allotted time in Peru. Still, when the superior arrived, I was nervous about expressing those opinions, thinking that he might see them as some sort of violation of the vow of obedience by this uppity young priest. I needn't have worried.

After listening to me go on a bit about wanting some say in my next assignment, the superior responded: "I'm trying to get 75 percent of our friars to do exactly what you have just done. I can't know what is best for each one of them or the ministries where they might best serve unless they tell me and we decide together about future placements." I came out of our meeting walking on air.

Those two quite different examples of how God's will is figured out, separated by just a few years, give a good picture of how far we have traveled in our understanding of obedience— whether vowed or not. Once it was entirely a question of doing what you were told—by a religious superior, spiritual director, pastor, bishop, pope. It was rightly called blind obedience and was considered, incredibly, a high virtue, at least in vowed religious life. The whole business of obedience was very neat and clear—be guided simply and solely by what your superiors tell you to do. If you do that, you won't have to worry about what

God wants. (It's true that there was always a footnote in the chapters on obedience saying that you weren't supposed to obey an order that went against your conscience. But I don't remember people talking much about conflicts of conscience around questions of obedience.)

When we look back on the days of blind obedience, it's almost impossible to imagine that we actually lived that way. An unquestioning, almost slavish acceptance of what was considered God's will, implemented in the decrees of people in authority, left precious little room for the work of the Spirit in the hearts and minds of those who saw obedience that way. My very wise superior nailed it exactly when he told me that day in Lima how there was no way he could know what was best for each us or what ministries we might be called to. He saw what most of us have come to see, that the Holy Spirit works through many channels besides strictly authoritarian ones. In fact, it's amazing to think that we went so far in the direction of such "top-down" obedience when our whole Catholic-Christian tradition was built on servant leadership: "You know how those who exercise authority among the Gentiles lord it over them; their great ones make their importance felt. It cannot be like that with you. Anyone among you who aspires to greatness must serve the rest, and whoever wants to rank first among you must serve the needs of all. Such is the case with the Son of Man who has come not to be served by others but to serve" (Mt 20:28). Being in authority as a religious superior, a pastor, bishop, spiritual director, pope should always mean a ministry of enabling the rest of us to figure out and follow the directions of the Holy Spirit. Fortunately, we have come to understand that obedience—vowed or not—is really a question of trying to do just that and that the guidance of the Spirit comes in a variety of ways. For sure, we still respect religious superiors or spiritual directors or pastors in our faith communities as helpers in knowing the Spirit's work in our lives. In fact, much of this chapter will reflect on this point—that the Spirit is uniquely at work today in official Catholic social teaching. But there are many other ways of knowing what God's Spirit invites us to do.

Channels for Discerning God's Will

Prayer

Personal, communal, and liturgical prayer are obviously help-ful ways to know God's will, and all of us have many stories of guidance through prayer. A friend of mine told me once about the circumstances of his return to the practice of the faith after some twenty years away. His wife had discovered a very open and welcoming eucharistic community, and out of curiosity my friend decided to go with her to Mass one Sunday. He said that as he stood there in the midst of the gathering, an intense feeling of having come back home swept over him and he broke down in tears of gratitude. He never looked back. Clearly his wife's prayer, the community's, and in the end his own brought him to that graced moment.

Friendship

Friends so often help us figure out what the Spirit has in mind for us. Those special people who sometimes know us better than we know ourselves can tell us things about us or call forth ini-tiatives we might never have considered on our own. It was a special friendship that helped spur the idea of an intentional faith community in the inner city of Washington DC. For twenty years now we have tried to live a modest lifestyle, pray and reflect with Bible and newspaper in hand, and work in a whole variety of ways for social change. With all of the ups and downs, false starts and, yes, failures that go with an effort like this one, our Assisi Community continues as a fairly successful attempt to live our way into something new and worthwhile. Literally dozens of women and men have been at Assisi for longer or shorter peri-ods, sharing as equals the nitty-gritty of daily life and dreams for a better world. We hear that beyond our walls many more who have visited us or heard about us have felt the influence of this modest effort of ours. After twenty years, it feels as though the Spirit has been with us. And it was a deep friendship that began it all—two of us who once said to each other, "we think we can do this; let's try."

Community

That short reflection on the experience of our Assisi Community leads to the obvious fact that we don't live our life in God apart from others. Community guides us as we try to move with the Spirit. It has been that way since Jesus chose the men and women who would be his community. In another chapter I'll look at the phenomenon of the intentional eucharistic communities that have emerged in the last few decades, especially in the United States. Here I want to mention one that I have been associated with for thirty years. It meets every Sunday for Eucharist, and over the years it has moved gradually but purposefully from a somewhat elitist group of Catholics whose principal interest was progressive and well-arranged liturgical celebrations to a vigorous engagement with issues of impoverishment, violence, discrimination, and their underlying causes. The group has set up action-reflection groups around issues of hunger, sexism, and American public policy; sponsored and supported immigrant families; taken a regular turn serving in a Washington DC soup kitchen; and contributed financially to a long list of organizations that press for social change.

Over the years this community has come to see the connection between what it does on Sunday and what is happening in the wider world the rest of each week. This development—conversion really—from a fairly inward-oriented group to one that takes on the world has been wonderful to watch. And, of course, within this communal movement toward an other-oriented spirituality every single member of the group has been inspired to make changes in his or her own life in behalf of a hurting world. All of this surely represents an attitude of obedience to God's Spirit.

Personal Experience

Yet another source for knowing God's will comes from our life experiences. Our family of origin, the environment in which we grew up, our educational opportunities (or lack of them), our work place, the current times, and the particular circumstances of our life—all of these give the Spirit the raw material to work with in directing each of us.

A dear friend of mine grew up in a comfortable, loving, middle-class family, went to quality schools, worked for a while at a high-paying job, and wound up as a suburban wife and mother with a very successful husband. On the outside she had the best of all worlds—living the so-called American dream. But she also found herself becoming more and more concerned about the social questions that began to crash in on her consciousness during the 1960s and 1970s—civil rights, the Vietnam War, U.S. policies toward Chile and later Central America, the California farm-workers' movement. Slowly, but consistently, she let her life be influenced by what she saw as her privileged status in the midst of these problem areas of our country and the world. As she says, the process was just a question of "taking the next right step," beginning with her own lifestyle and that of her family. Today, thirty-plus years later, she finds herself 180 degrees from where she started, living modestly and finding fulfillment in a range of activities around the most pressing issues of this time in our history—globalization and its effects on the poor, world debt, peaceful solutions to international problems, and so forth. Hers is a clear example of the Spirit guiding a good-willed person of faith in and through and past some fairly typical experiences of modern American life—and of her obedience to that guidance. Her six children, too, have found their own ways of making a better world for those less fortunate than they are.

My best friend during the years I spent in Peru worked as a structural engineer. He designed high-rise buildings that could withstand the constant tremors and occasional earthquakes that are so common in that part of the world, and he made a lot of money. When it looked like the deadly terrorist organization Sendero Luminoso (Shining Path) would take over Peru in the 1980s and early 1990s, my friend knew that prominent and well-to-do people would be particular targets of this anarchist regime. In fact his wife once shared with me her fear that her husband "could wind up dead in the trunk of his car." As things became more and more desperate in Peru, I called him one day and asked if he had ever considered taking his family to live in a safer place—something that was certainly within his means. I found his answer absolutely courageous and a Spirit-inspired response in obedience to a defining life experience. He said to me: "Jose, I'm making a Bonhoeffer choice to stay in Peru." That, of course, was a reference to the great Lutheran pastor Dietrich von Bonhoeffer, who rejected the opportunity to leave Hitler's Germany in the 1930s and eventually lost his life in a Nazi concentration camp. (Fortunately, the leader of Sendero Luminoso, Abimael Guzman, was captured before his terrorist cohorts got to Lima. The movement collapsed, and my friend was spared.)

Signs of the Times

Reading the signs of the times to find out what the Spirit wills for us comes right out of the gospel. Jesus said it this way: "In the evening you say, 'Red sky at night, the day will be bright'; but in the morning, 'Sky red and gloomy, the day will be stormy.' If you know how to interpret the look of the sky, can you not read the signs of the times?" (Mt 16:4). When the elderly Pope John XXIII made the startling announcement on Christmas Day, 1961, that he would convoke a general council of the church, he used that very text from Matthew and its clear challenge for us to be on the lookout for the inspiration of God's Holy Spirit in the circumstances of current history. In *Humanae Salutis* the pope wrote: "We make our own the recommendation of Jesus that one should know how to distinguish the 'signs of the times.' . . . We considered that the times now were right to offer to the Catholic Church and to the world the gift of a new Ecumenical Council."

In 1968, three years after the close of the Second Vatican Council, the Catholic bishops of Latin America got together to look at the realities of their world in the light of what they had heard and done during the council. People who read what the Latin American bishops came up with marvel at what they said—for example, calling the whole Latin American church to stand with the poor and insisting that the church itself had to be "of the poor." Where did these prelates get such radical notions, and, perhaps more tellingly, where did they find the courage to demand those kinds of changes of themselves and of the rest of their church communities? I find one answer to that question simple and convincing: most bishops in Latin America had frequent and direct contact with the poor. It was unavoidable. Most people who live in Latin America are poor. Those firsthand experiences of grinding, dehumanizing poverty provided fertile ground for the Spirit to work with the bishops as they thought about council statements like the opening words of the *Pastoral Constitution on the Church in the Modern World:* "The joys and hopes, the fears and anxieties of the men of this time, especially those who are poor or in any way afflicted, these too are the joys and hopes, the fears and anxieties of the followers of Christ." The Latin American bishops let the Spirit lead them in the light of the realities—signs of the time—that they saw all around them. And the results were phenomenal for the whole church there.

I've often thought that the North American church needs the same kind of breakthrough experience based on the signs of our times. The list of problem areas where our country exercises enormous influence—sometimes for good, often for harm—and that cry out for a gospel response is endless. One example: as the United States prepared for its preemptive invasion of Iraq in 2002 and 2003, Pope John Paul II spoke out against such a war. He made the famous observation that "war is a defeat for humanity." Yet how many Catholic Americans heard from their pulpits anything about the pope's views? There was a (literally) deafening silence in the churches of this country around our tragically ill-advised strike at Iraq. Had our church at some point done the same kind of social analysis on American reality that the bishops of Latin America did on theirs after Vatican II, I believe we all would have been ready to hear warnings like John Paul's and perhaps averted the disaster the Iraq War has produced. "If you know how to interpret the look of the sky, can you not read the signs of the times?" (Mt 16:4).

A New Grace

That reflection on the signs of the times as one sure way of figuring out where the Spirit is leading us at any given moment takes us to a relatively new and quite powerful channel for discernment. The church's social teaching over the past century has swept over the Catholic community and pointed out clearly the will of God for each of us and for humanity as a whole. We've never before had such a rich and broad-gauged body of teaching about almost every social issue that confronts the world, precisely because there has never been a moment in history like ours. In fact, Catholic social teaching has been called a new grace of the Spirit. Beginning in 1891, when Pope Leo XIII wrote the first modern social encyclical, entitled *On the Reconstruction of the Social Order (Rerum Novarum),* the Holy Spirit has gifted the church and the world with dozens of official and semi-official reflections and guidelines for just about every aspect of modern life. Below, we'll list the most important of these documents, and just their titles will indicate their far-reaching scope. But first a word needs to be said about the phrase *new grace.*

New graces have always come to the church and world as times have changed. The great debate in the infant church of Jerusalem about whether Gentiles had to be converted to Judaism before becoming Christians resulted in a new grace. The "apostles and presbyters, in agreement with the whole Jerusalem church" sent a letter to the "brothers of Gentile origin in Antioch, Syria, and Cilicia" that said: "It is the decision of the Holy Spirit, and ours too, not to lay on you any burden beyond that which is strictly necessary" (Acts 15:22, 23, 28). It is interesting to speculate about what would have happened had the church in Jerusalem not obeyed the Spirit and had instead rejected that new grace. Imagine the sort of confusing messages that would have been sent by insistence on a Jewish ritual before baptism into Christ.

A new grace appeared in the early centuries of the Christian era when individuals responded to the Spirit and began living intense lives of prayer in the desert. They were a new grace at that time, forerunners in the Catholic-Christian world of the great tradition of religious orders. Out of these early experiences came the monastic life of St. Benedict and his blood sister St. Scholastica—a new grace at a time when Western civilization had come apart (the so-called Dark Ages). For centuries this new grace operated in and through the Benedictine monasteries, which kept learning alive and served as centers where people could come for material and spiritual nourishment.

As the rigid feudal system in Europe began to crumble in the thirteenth and fourteenth centuries and cities began to emerge, bringing with them entrepreneurship and the beginning of capitalism, the mendicant movements of the Franciscans and the Dominicans appeared. These "street monks" moved into the marketplaces of that world, witnessing to the victims of this new order of things—the poor, the lepers, the outcasts. Obviously, the mendicants were a new grace of the Spirit, crucial for a world starting to divide into "haves" and "have nots."

The vigorous Jesuit order, led by its charismatic founder, Ignatius of Loyola, emerged in the sixteenth century. The Jesuits' intelligent, Spirit-led processes of "discernment of spirits" provided a new grace for a church that had lost its way because of corruption and luxury. The Jesuits were the Roman Catholic response to the Protestant Reformation. And as modern societies and nation-states continued to take shape in the seventeenth, eighteenth, and nineteenth centuries, with their fallout of neglected, forgotten, and abandoned people, thousands of lay and religious groups stepped in to provide schools and hospitals and orphanages for those impoverished people. These groups became a tidal wave of apostolic religious congregations—new graces for new times.

The Second Vatican Council itself was a new grace. Where would the church be today had not Pope John read the signs of our times and had the council not responded with the breakthrough in thinking expressed in documents like the *Pastoral Constitution on the Church in the Modern World, Declaration on Religious Freedom,* and *Declaration on the Relation of the Church to Non-Christian Religions*? Forty years after that amazing event in Catholic-Christian history, we still have a long way to go in understanding the opportunities and challenges this particular new grace holds out for the household of faith and the world. What a shame, then, that certain powerful forces in the Catholic community are trying to undercut and repress the spirit of Vatican II. Where is their faith in the Holy Spirit, who constantly calls the church to move forward into the history unfolding around and within it?

So it's clear that our faith community has always received new graces from God as times have changed and new circumstances have presented themselves. And it's no surprise that this very different and challenging modern age should also benefit from a new grace. It was to be expected. As the twentieth century proceeded and humanity experienced incredibly rapid means of transportation, instant communications, economic and social interdependence across the world, and amazingly, looked at our planet from outer space, new graces had to come. This globalization (the extension of the effects of modernity to the entire world and the compression of time and space—all coming at the same time), demanded a gospel word. The Spirit has provided it in the social teaching of the Catholic Church.

Social Statements

A list of the titles of some major documents that make up the principal social teaching of the church proves the claim that we have here a new grace, as well as a call from the Spirit for a spirituality that supports this dimension of gospel life:

1891   *On the Condition of Labor*

1931   *The Reconstruction of the Social Order*

1961   *Christianity and Social Progress*

1963   *Peace on Earth*

1965   *Pastoral Constitution on the Church in the Modern World*

1967   *On the Development of Peoples*

1971   *Justice in the World*

1971   *A Call to Action*

1975   *Evangelization in the Modern World*

1979   *Redeemer of Humankind*

1981   *On Human Work*

1988   *The Social Concerns of the Church*

1988   *The Church and Racism*

1990   *The Missionary Activity of the Church*

1991	*One Hundred Years [of Catholic Social Teaching]*
1992	*The Catechism of the Catholic Church*
1995	*The Gospel of Life*
2001	*Contribution to World Conference against Racism, Xeno-phobia, and Related Intolerance*

We've had similar documents on social issues from various regions of the Catholic-Christian world as well. Just to name a few:

1968	*The Church in the Present-Day Transformation of Latin America in the Light of the Council* (Latin American Episcopal Conference)
1981	*Justice and Evangelization* (Symposium of Episcopal Conferences of Africa)
1983	*The Challenge of Peace: God's Promise and Our Response* (U.S. bishops)
1996	*The Common Good and the Catholic Church's Social Teaching* (Catholic Bishops' Conference of England and Wales)
2000	*A Renewed Church in Asia: A Mission of Love and Service* (Asian bishops)

Scanning this quite amazing and consistent emphasis on social questions in the twentieth and twenty-first centuries shows us that issues of social justice, peace, human rights, and global solidarity have come front and center in Catholic-Christian thought. This large body of social teaching surely adds up to a new grace of the Holy Spirit for our times, one that any authentic Catholic-Christian spirituality has to take into consideration. That really is the point of this whole book. I believe that the Spirit is crying out for us to know about and act on the social issues that have pushed their way onto humanity's radar screen.

Religious Life and Obedience to This New Grace

I hope it is clear that I believe all new graces come from the Spirit to the entire church—lay, religious, clergy—and indeed to

all people of good will. As an older vowed religious I have the
experience to reflect deeply on the implications of this new grace
for my sisters and brothers in religious life. However, no one is
exempt from obedience to these graces, and I encourage everyone
who reads these lines to apply a similar discernment to his or her
particular life situation. Here I single out those women and men
in our faith community who have felt called to make public vows
in religious orders and congregations, because it does seem that
these new graces have a particular claim on them.

We just ran through a brief overview of the new graces show-
ered on the church and world right from the beginning of the
Christian era and how Holy Spirit called forth new forms of
vowed life (the Benedictine tradition, the Franciscan and Do-
minican movements, the Jesuits and apostolic congregations)
when these were needed. Now a new call from the Spirit rings
through the church and religious life—engagement with the way
our world is organized. Members of today's religious congregations are in a unique position to respond to this new grace. I believe that the very future of what some people call consecrated
life—vowed life—in the church hangs on the ability of its members to take up that response as it is laid out in Catholic social
teaching.

Think about the radical freedom that vowed women and men
should have through obedience, poverty, and celibate chastity. I
believe religious publicly profess a personal willingness and readi-
ness to embrace the new challenges set out in the social teaching
of the church. And in line with the new grace of Catholic social
teaching virtually all religious orders and congregations in formal
and official ways have called their members in recent years to
that same commitment. Increasingly, the various levels of religious communities—local house meetings, regional days, canoni-
cal chapters on the provincial and worldwide levels—have made
their own the prophetic words of the 1971 document *Justice in the
World:* "Action on behalf of justice and participation in the transformation of the world fully appear to us [bishops] as constitu-
tive of the preaching of the Gospel" (no. 6). My own Franciscan
province based in New York City has called all of us friars to look
at each of our ministries as well as our lives as brothers in community through the lens of globalization. In a recent official meeting we also described ourselves as "preemptive peacemakers"—an

obvious reference and challenge to America's claiming the right to start a "preemptive war."

In addition, vowed religious have in their collective memories the history of those orders and congregations that have always responded to new graces. We noted above that as modern societies developed and the gaps between poverty and privilege became wider, religious men, and especially religious women, established much-needed orphanages, nursing homes, hospitals, and schools for the poor. That wonderful legacy continues today as the sisters, brothers, and priests of the various orders and congregations, particularly in the so-called Third World, do the new work for social change. They ask and act on modern questions like: After all these centuries why do orphanages and hospitals and schools for the poor continue to be necessary? What structures can we put in place so that everyone gets a fair share of the opportunities available to the rest? Why can't we settle our national and international differences peacefully, without resorting to military options? Is there any way to "level the playing field" for poor nations in relation to wealthy ones?

What's more, religious vows strike me as tickets to the fearsome vocation of prophet. If we accept that we have a new grace in Catholic social teaching, then the prophetic task today means speaking out and acting on the various social problems facing humanity—world hunger, wealth and poverty existing side by side, racism, sexism, classism, militarism, violations of the environment, the need for world government, the need to curb transnational corporations. The list is seemingly endless. I believe that religious can no longer reduce and confine their ministries to individual problems alone, though these are important. The Spirit calls us loudly and clearly to engage with the way our societies are set up, because basically they are set up against the poor.

The good news is that many individual religious have willingly accepted this new grace, and it has given renewed meaning to their personal lives and life in their congregations. The bad news is that despite great written statements and resolutions to this effect, many religious and religious congregations have yet to place this new grace at the very center of their ministries and their life in common. Still, all members of religious orders and congregations have the inspiration and the room in their lives to do just that. What is required is the will to do it—a large order for those of us who live in this world of ease and individualism. The empire gives us no help in living in obedience to the new grace of social engagement. In fact, that way of living represents a counter-cultural mindset and lifestyle that make the empire very nervous. It can't stand for its subjects to make their own decisions, to question its priorities and policies, or to march to a different drummer—as religious by definition are supposed to do. The challenge of obedience goes beyond the individual who vows it; obedience to the Spirit confronts the church, the nation, and the world. And that's a very good definition of prophecy and the prophetic call.

I said above that the very future of what we know as religious life hangs on the ability of its members to take up this response. Let me begin to draw this reflection of obedience to a close with one dramatic example that emphasizes both the call that this new grace of social involvement represents for religious communities and how crucial it is for them to answer it. Some years ago a leader in one particular congregation asked me to visit all the houses and ministries of his order in the United States. The roots of this particular group were caring for the sick poor. For centuries, literally, its members had faithfully carried on this work, and their communities had flourished. But somewhere in mid-twentieth-century America the costs of our sophisticated, high-tech medicine overtook that charism, and the brothers decided it was essential to fill the beds in their hospitals with paying customers. Inevitably, the sick poor got squeezed out of their ministries. In time, vocations to the congregation fell off, as prospective candidates wondered what difference there was between the work of these religious and any other for-profit health organization. A general malaise began to seep into the community's life, a feeling that perhaps it was all over for them.

My job was to look at this situation and see if some change of course was possible. I decided that the best place to start my visits was with the statements these religious had made about themselves—their mission goals. I compared these to their balance sheets and found—surprise, surprise—that the two did not match. What they said so eloquently about their tradition of ministry to the sick poor—people who could not pay for the care these religious provided—was totally contradicted by the reality of those who were actually receiving that care—people who *could* pay for it. When I finished my visits to their houses and hospitals, I had to tell the men what I truly felt—that I didn't see much hope for their survival. I said that the decline in new vocations together with a general feeling of discontent within the community seemed clearly to be the result of having lost sight of their founding vision. Happily, I was wrong.

When the HIV/AIDS epidemic swept across the United States in the 1980s, these religious saw an opportunity to remake themselves. They began to take in people who were infected with the virus and to specialize in treating these modern outcasts. While the final results of this turnabout won't be seen for years to come, there are signs already that this congregation is revitalized. Whatever the final outcome for this group, the lesson I take from this admittedly anecdotal and limited experience is that religious life clearly stands or falls according to how it answers the call of the Spirit at this moment of salvation history—a call that sounds loud and clear in Catholic social teaching. The same is true at every level of church life—parish, diocese, prayer group, Bible study circle—you name it.

Some time ago two members of our Assisi Community in Washington were part of a Pax Christi (the Catholic peace movement) delegation to Colombia. While there, they visited a diocese in one of the most dangerous areas of that country. The local bishop and priests routinely engaged in extremely risky activities on behalf of human rights—standing up for poor people threatened by the deadly forces of the army, the guerrillas and the paramilitary in that tortured country. What most impressed our people was the large number of young men studying for the priesthood in that diocese. The bishop said that he had enough vocations to place two priests in every parish under his care. This is one more telling example that the vitality of the church depends directly on its obedience—or lack thereof—to the Spirit's new graces, the more challenging the better.

Conclusion

A final word about obedience and the Holy Spirit.

At a particularly critical moment in his life, Jesus left us some consoling thoughts regarding the work of the Spirit in our lives and in the world. When he took his last meal with friends the night of his capture, torture and execution, he spoke about his impending departure from them in words his hearers later remembered and wrote down in detail. We read, "The Paraclete, the Holy Spirit whom the Father will send in my name, will instruct you in everything, and remind you of all that I told you" (Jn 14:26). And again, "When the Paraclete comes, the Spirit of truth who comes from the Father—and whom I myself will send from the Father—he will bear witness on my behalf" (Jn 15:26). And yet again: "It is much better for you that I go. If I fail to go, the Paraclete will never come to you, whereas if I go, I will send him to you. . . . When he comes, however, being the Spirit of truth he will guide you to all truth. He will not speak on his own, but will speak only what he hears and will announce to you the things to come" (Jn 16:7, 13).

In looking at all of the new graces God has given us to deal with the ever-changing circumstances history sets before people of faith and good will, these promises of Jesus that we will always have a guiding Spirit ring true. They must have proved enormously consoling and energizing for the disciples who first heard them, as they watched his brutal death and, then, a short time later, when he left his work in their hands. They knew at the first Pentecost that Jesus had kept his word about the help of the Spirit, because these timid, frightened recluses burst out of their hideaway on that day and began the work of preaching Christ Crucified to the ends of the earth. People like Benedict and Scholastica, Francis and Clare, Dominic and Ignatius, Teresa and John of the Cross, John XXIII, Dorothy Day, and Oscar Romero must also have felt the power of the promised Advocate. Where else would they have gotten the audacity to do the bold things they did? Today, we have the same assurance from the Lord, as the Spirit continues to challenge, console, inspire and direct the work of furthering God's reign on earth through us—flawed human beings. Our task, just like that of every person of faith throughout history, is clear—to recognize the graces given for our times and to respond to them in obedience.

Chapter 6

• • • • •

Poverty and Chastity

From the beginning it's important to say that, like obedience, the virtues of poverty and chastity stand as values that all Christian spirituality takes seriously. They're not just for people who feel called to a religious, vowed life. The poverty that breaks the backs of millions of people around the world today and the madness of our culture with regard to questions of sexual morality and personal integrity, I'm convinced, call for a countervailing witness to poverty and chastity on the part of good-willed and faith-filled people. So, while this chapter makes a lot of references to the vows of poverty and celibate chastity that members of religious orders make, they apply equally to every person of good will.

Some years ago I attended the final profession ceremony for several young Franciscans of my province, at which they took lifetime vows of poverty, chastity, and obedience. It was a dramatic moment for them and for all of us who were there. Our provincial superior at the time gave the homily, a nice reflection on the profession of vows, well prepared, sincere, and preached with conviction. But as I listened to his comments on the importance of the step these young men were taking, I felt myself squirming a bit. Something, I thought, wasn't quite right. There was something missing.

It was only later, during the train ride home, that I put my finger on what it was that bothered me about our superior's homily. His words lacked any historical context—at least as I had heard them. The message could have been preached in 1930 or

1960 or 1980. The thoughts he expressed were good, progressive reflections on religious vows, but they made no mention of the here-and-now social, political, and cultural environment in which these public promises of poverty, chastity, and obedience were being made. Nothing was said about why these several young American men would take such a radical step in the world of today and nothing about the impact their profession of vows could and ought to make on a society like the United States. The homily was totally ahistorical at a time and in a place where, I felt, a here-and-now context was all-important.

Another time I was talking with a brother Franciscan whom I knew to be a good man and serious about his life as a vowed religious. The subject of poverty came up, and to my amazement he told me that he could think of no reason why anyone in modern America would take such a vow. Here was a dedicated person of faith who couldn't explain to himself or to others why he carried around a public vow of poverty.

As the dreadful clerical scandal came to light a few years ago, I found myself remembering some of the bizarre thinking about celibate chastity that circulated during the post–Vatican II years of the 1960s and 1970s, when, we've learned, a lot of the predatory activities by priests took place. One story in particular that came to mind was about a priest who rationalized his sexual encounters by claiming that his vow of celibacy meant simply and solely that he was not to marry—nothing more! These aberrations, of course, can be traced to an earlier "understanding" of and perhaps a reaction to celibate chastity as a denial and rejection of all that is sexual. People went so far as to declare that they were putting sex "on the shelf" the moment they made their vow of celibate chastity. A sure recipe for later problems.

Those stories give us an entry point for this chapter on poverty and chastity. I believe that both the "what" and the "why" of these vows are important. But if I had to decide which to emphasize, it would be the why. What rationale at the beginning of the twenty-first century in the so-called developed world explains why normal, intelligent women and men promise to live a life of poverty and celibate chastity? In the profession homily I spoke of above, there was no mention of why the vows are relevant to modern life. In that conversation I had with my brother friar, he displayed an astounding ignorance of anything that would make sense of a vow of poverty in America today. And a priest who could write off celibate chastity as merely a prohibition on marriage exhibits no understanding of the deep personal commitment that vow entails, much less its consequences for U.S. culture. I believe being able to articulate the relevancy—to answer the *why* question—of poverty and celibate chastity is crucial both for the vowed person and for society. As a very wise and experienced religious once said, "If we don't have a convincing reason for living these vows today, they can tend to destroy us."

Poverty

Let's be clear up front that the kind of poverty which is lived by all too many people in our world is an evil and a scandal, something to be fought against and overcome whenever and wherever possible. That is a central argument in this book on spirituality. The remarkable international, national, and local initiatives that try to lessen and eliminate the grinding poverty still suffered by too many in our world are much-needed graces of the Holy Spirit. The great liberation theologian Gustavo Gutiérrez says it this way: "Material poverty is a subhuman situation. . . . Concretely, to be poor means to die of hunger, to be illiterate, to be exploited by others, not to know that you are being exploited, not to know that you are a person."[1] Quite simply, poverty is an evil.

Pope Paul VI, in his 1967 social encyclical *On the Development of Peoples*, is equally explicit. Speaking of human development, which he says is the movement from less human to more human conditions of life, the pope writes: "Less human conditions first affect those who are so poor as to lack the minimum essentials for life; . . . then they affect those who are oppressed by social structures which have been created by abuses of ownership or by abuses of power, by the exploitation of the workers or by unfair business deals. . . . More human conditions of life clearly imply passage from want to the possession of necessities" (no. 21). Overcoming poverty is a duty.

Those reflections on material poverty make the clear point that there is no sense in which such poverty can be glorified or spiritualized. We're all called to get rid of whatever stands in the way of full human life, and poverty surely does that. So the questions are these: In what sense does our Catholic-Christian tradition hold out poverty as a virtue? Why on earth would people feel called to take a vow of poverty or to live a simple lifestyle? Some rationale, please!

Poverty Embraced

A Sane Lifestyle

In the first place, on a purely human level, without any particular reference to faith or religious motivation, a simple lifestyle, relative and voluntary poverty, is clearly a better way to live. Experience shows that choosing to have fewer of this world's goods, results in a freer and more unencumbered life. We don't have the many worries we hear from the affluent about losing things or getting robbed. On a worldwide scale, it is clearer than ever today that the very survival of our physical world requires a simpler way of living, especially on the part of those of us who live in the developed, industrialized world; the earth cannot much longer support our endless, superfluous wants. Just looking at the results of America's addiction to oil proves the point.

Some years ago I lived in community with four young women and men who were volunteering two years of their lives to help in a variety of social ministries—a soup kitchen, a crisis-intervention center, outreach to at-risk children. The simple lifestyles of these young adults taught me a lesson. Each of them seemed to take for granted that cars were an unnecessary luxury and instead used public transportation for their work and recreation. A vegetarian diet was standard in the household, because, as they told me, it took too much grain to produce each pound of meat. They believed that one "dressy" outfit was quite enough for special occasions; otherwise, clean tee-shirts and jeans sufficed. Even though each of these volunteers was a person of faith, I didn't notice that their lifestyle choices were directly inspired

by the gospel. They seemed to understand instinctively that, as
the saying goes, they should live simply so others could simply
live. That attitude strikes me as a first and very good reason for
practicing a kind of poverty (which in most other areas of the
world would not be seen as poverty at all). It also narrows the
gap between people who have much more than enough and their
sisters and brothers who live in shelters or frequent soup kitchens. Living with less is a better and saner way of living, and it
does not insult those who *must* live with less because they have
no choice in the matter.

Traditional Reasons for Religious Poverty

As we look for a faith-inspired reason to make a vow of poverty, something connected with Jesus and our Catholic-Christian
faith, one traditional explanation inevitably comes to mind: in
giving up all claims to owning anything, vowed religious make a
statement about their complete dependence on God for everything. The gospel inspiration for this view of poverty goes all the
way back to the Beatitudes in Matthew's Gospel: "Blessed are the
poor in spirit, for theirs is the kingdom of heaven" (Mt 5:3). This
vow to rely on God for every material need, often called spiritual
poverty, is still a valid rationale for this vow. But there are some
pitfalls around it too.

Spiritual poverty can be used to cover up a lifestyle that is
anything but spare or austere. Sometimes (many times?) it comes
out like this among vowed religious: "I depend on God for everything—and by God I'm going to have everything." Religious today get criticized as people who take the vow of poverty while
other people live it. The sheer wealth of many religious orders
and congregations, especially in the United States, the comfort
and security that surround religious, and increasingly our sense
of entitlement make many people, including religious, wonder
about this "total dependence on God" business. The lifestyle of
vowed religious today may be understandable in a world where
having more money or things is a measure of who the person is;
where conspicuous consumption is a way of life; where "going
shopping" is a normal and frequent recreational activity. We may
hide behind the rationale of spiritual poverty, but it's phony. In

the midst of this American culture of excess we surely need a more convincing rationale for living this vow, one that is relevant for this time and place, something more solid than the shaky ground of "spiritual poverty." Here are three reasons that speak to me.

Witness

The vow of poverty, lived with integrity, witnesses to a world in which some people live extraordinarily affluent and privileged lives while most people lack the basic necessities even for survival. Poverty, as a conscious and ongoing choice, is a much-needed, prophetic statement in this empire that doesn't seem upset at all by the global divide between the "haves" and the "have nots." The vowed person says with his or her life, "I choose to have less because my sisters and brothers have nothing." In that way poverty is a social vow, a social commitment. An example from my own life may help illustrate the point.

As a young boy and teen-ager growing up in Boston, I played a lot of ice hockey. Those cold New England winters made "the pond" a place where all of us kids gathered every chance we could. Later, as an adult, I took a lot of pleasure in ice-skating. On the first Christmas after my return to the United States following fifteen years in Latin America, my family gave me an expensive pair of skates. Their present put my Christmas under the cloud of a real dilemma: could I accept this loving gesture on the family's part with my still fresh memory of people I had known by name in Latin America for whom the price of those skates was more money than they might see in a year? For several days I went back and forth over the question and finally decided that I had to return the skates and ask my family members to please understand why I could not take their thoughtful and well-meaning gift. In fact, I included a letter of explanation as I turned over the skates.

To this day I'm not sure if I did the right thing—though I know I made the best decision possible for me at the time—or if my relatives ever understood my reasoning. However, shortly afterward one of my cousins, who had contributed to the purchase of the ice skates, told me an interesting story. She was doing some post-Christmas shopping in an upscale department store in Boston and noticed a display of expensive tote bags. To draw attention to the merchandise, the decorators had placed the bags around a papier-mâché figure of a homeless woman, a street person. My cousin went straight to the manager of the store and complained that the display was an insult to the poor, and that if it stayed there she would never again darken the door of his establishment. In record time, she told me, the papier-mâché figure was gone. While my cousin did not explicitly make the connection, I like to think that my problem with expensive ice skates had something to do with her reaction to mocking the poor for marketing purposes. Witnessing to human poverty makes a statement and has an effect. For me, that's a compelling rationale for voluntary and/or vowed poverty.

Solidarity

Another motivation for the vow of poverty that speaks to me has to do with solidarity with those who have no choice in life but impoverishment. They're born into it, suffer it every day of their lives, and die in it. In trying to live with less by letting go of all the superfluous and superficial consumer items that life in the United States throws at us, by insisting that we don't need nearly so much "stuff," we put ourselves on the side of the real poor. We live out a preferential option for the poor, something that has become a central part of Catholic-Christian spirituality today. Said another way, in choosing and practicing poverty, we make decisions on a daily basis and in a whole variety of ways not to insult the poor by the way we live.

St. Francis of Assisi once taught a lesson in this regard when he spoke about what perfect joy is all about. This is, of course, a thirteenth-century story with all of the cultural differences we would expect at a distance of eight hundred years. But, like so many other things in the life of this "saint for all times," the story holds a core of truth that can serve us today. St. Francis said, "When we come to St. Mary of the Angels, soaked by the rain and frozen by the cold, all soiled with mud and suffering from hunger, and we ring at the gate of the place and the brother porter comes and says angrily: 'Who are you?' And we say: 'We are two of your brothers.' And he contradicts us, saying: 'you are not telling the truth. Rather you are two rascals who go around deceiving people and stealing what they give to the poor. Go away!' And he does not open for us, but makes us stand outside in the snow and rain, cold and hungry, until night falls—then if we endure all those insults and cruel rebuffs patiently, without being troubled and without complaining, and if we reflect humbly and charitably that that porter really knows us and that God makes him speak against us, oh Brother Leo, write that perfect joy is there!"[2]

The point of this lesson, I believe, has something to do with our modern idea of solidarity. Francis felt that being treated as a poor person, being mistaken for one, even by a fellow friar, was "perfect joy." He had reached such a sublime point in his own conversion process where his option for the poor showed itself when others saw and treated him as a poor person. The story has interesting and challenging consequences when we think about how poor people are treated today—begging on city streets, herded into shelters, rebuffed at the desks of bureaucrats. A vow of poverty or commitment to a simple lifestyle can in analogous ways place us in similar circumstances as we consciously forego claims to privilege and power.

I've spoken about our Assisi community life in the inner city of Washington DC. We chose to live in a poor neighborhood to be in solidarity with the rest of the folks there. Over the years I've noticed that we do share their poverty in some surprising ways. Garbage collection, for example, is hurried, and lots of refuse is left on the ground after it spills (something upscale neighborhoods won't stand for). Taxi drivers have refused to come into our area after dark, and for years a drug trade flourished on our streets as suburban users came for their fixes knowing that the police weren't likely to show up in that area of the city. Once, when a friend of mine came for a visit, he kept looking out the window to make sure his new car was safe. In our community's choice of where to live we've found that solidarity with the poor comes at you if you put yourself in its way.

Sharing in the Paschal Mystery

Finally, for me, the ultimate rationale for poverty centers on Jesus and the cross. This connection is theological, even mystical. I first heard it from liberation theologian Gustavo Gutiérrez,

and over the years it has made increasing sense to me. Basically
it goes like this: Our faith tells us that Jesus overcame sin and its
consequences through his suffering, death, and resurrection. To
try to live the virtue of poverty is to do, in a specific way, what
Jesus did when he let himself be taken prisoner and crucified.

Let's try to unpack that.

Why God chose this way to redeem humanity goes to the heart
of the matter, the central question around Christ's role in salvation history. Many books have been written that try to shed light
on this mystery. For me, the best attempt comes from Jesuit theologian Jon Sobrino. What he says about the reasons for Jesus'
death is absolutely relevant to the profound connection between
the Paschal Mystery and voluntary poverty: "Over against the
notion of God as power Jesus sets the notion of God as love. . . .
Jesus' universal love takes different concrete forms, depending on
the situation. He manifests his love for the oppressed by being
with them, by offering them something that might restore their
dignity and make them truly human. He manifests his love for
the oppressors by being against them, by trying to strip away all
that is making them less than human. In short, Jesus' love is
political because it is situated in the concrete. And that conception of political love led him perforce to the cross. . . . We see that
the cross of Jesus cannot be properly understood and appreciated
unless we view it in terms of Jesus' whole life. His life is a journey that leads to the cross. . . . The cross is not the result of some
divine decision independent of history; it is the outcome of the
basic option for incarnation in a given situation. That entails
conflict, because sin holds power in history and takes the triumphant form of religious and political oppression. Jesus had to
choose between evading all that or facing up to it squarely. He
chose the latter course, challenging the idolatrous use of power
to oppress people and the idolatrous conception of God that justified such use."[3]

In all of the literature and argumentation, one central fact remains clear: that Jesus' suffering, dying and rising is the way
salvation happened—"did not the Messiah have to undergo all
these things in order to enter his glory?" (Lk 24:26). As Sobrino
indicates, Jesus took on our real-life, historical poverty in order
to lift us out of it; he "became sin," as St. Paul says, to save us

from sin. So, in the face of this incredible truth that stands at the very heart of the mystery of Jesus' redemptive suffering and death, a person who lives a vow of poverty and/or purposely takes on a spare lifestyle does what St. Paul claimed when he said, "I fill up what is lacking in the sufferings of Christ" (Col 1:24). That person takes on human poverty (fills up what is lacking in the sufferings of Christ) and, if St. Paul is right, connects with Jesus' saving action. A choice for poverty is personal and individual, but it is social and political as well—just as Jesus' dying was.

This is all very deep and mystical. There isn't much logic to it. Connecting through poverty with Jesus on Calvary is an act of faith. And it's best to leave it there for each one's personal consideration. But I believe it is worth serious thought and reflection because this conjoining of a commitment to poverty with Jesus' cross comes very close to the heart of what it means to follow him. It is the deepest and, in the end, the most compelling rationale for making a commitment to poverty.

Poverty in the Empire

Whatever the rationale for living with less that best speaks to each of us, there is no doubt that the ones who make that choice are a challenge, yes, a threat to powerful forces that pull in the opposite direction. We had a vivid example of that pull when the priorities of the empire were thrown in our faces right after 9/11. The president of the United States assured us that he would make sure we took revenge on our enemies and advised us to *go out shopping*. What an incredible and insulting piece of advice to give in response to an unspeakable tragedy! Go out and get more stuff, spend money, make yourselves feel good, keep this capitalist monster fed. And this at a moment when, in a society that prides itself on being "of the people, by the people, and for the people," we should have been engaging in a nationwide debate on what provoked those attacks and what would be the most reasonable course of action in response. Think of the logic of poverty in that scenario. It calls into question and subverts the entire framework of imperialism.

The empire promises us security. Its current leaders have recently taken us into two wars half a world away so that "we won't have to fight terrorism in our own streets." Now, more than five years later, with tens of thousands of lives lost and hundreds of billions spent, the empire and the rest of the world are not more secure but less so. In the face of that colossal failure the security that comes from wanting and having less looks a lot more solid to me.

The empire has to search out new markets for its corporate overproduction in agriculture, manufactured goods, pharmaceuticals, and services (banks, insurance, information). The United States, for example, is selling its corn to Mexico at a cheap price, and Mexican corn growers are going out of business because they cannot compete in their own markets. The empire has to get people to buy not only what they need but also what they want, even when they can't afford those wants. What's happening is that wants are expanding and the basic needs of people across the globe are not being met. Over against such a top-heavy and bankrupt system, a mentality of poverty seems like a reasonable and hope-filled alternative.

But the empire doesn't appreciate opposition. It's considered unpatriotic (un-American), marginal, even kooky to suggest that anything but enthusiasm for the consumerist mentality of ever-expanding markets is the way to go. So a spirit of poverty becomes a prophetic way of living in the heart of the empire. It says to the capitalist system, "You have no clothes." Poverty and simple living are very rational ways to organize one's life.

Chastity and Celibacy

Chastity is a value, like poverty, that every person of faith has to hold. It's part of the commandment to love our neighbor as we love ourselves. We're speaking here of integrity, respect, and care in sexual matters on the part of single lay people, married couples, and vowed religious. The only difference is that religious commit themselves to celibacy as well.

Once again I want to propose the real questions: Why chastity? What rationale best helps us to live a life of integrity and respect for our own and others' dignity and rights in sexual matters? Why are some people called to live this value as celibates? Again, it's the *why* that is crucial to ask today, when popular culture in the empire has pretty much lost its way in the area of human sexuality. The following rationales help me.

A Witness of Personal Integrity

It seems clear that chastity and celibacy are values that have a whole lot to do with personal integrity. In trying to live them, the individual projects a sense of respect for his or her own person and the person of everyone else. A sad example may help to show how much we need this basic rationale for chastity.

Some years ago I met a middle-aged man who wanted to talk with me about a problem he was having. In the course of our conversation he casually mentioned that he was involved in an affair with a married woman. When I questioned him about this, he seemed surprised that I would make anything of it, telling me that neither he nor the woman were very happily married and so no one was being hurt. I tried to point out that because of the affair the other woman's husband was being hurt, that he was hurting his own wife and their shaky marriage, and finally, that he was sacrificing his integrity—surely hurting himself. I never saw him again. If that is a snapshot of how casually and superficially sexuality is treated today—and from experience I believe it is—then our culture desperately needs many, many faithful women and men, married and single, lay and religious, who live chaste lives of personal and mutual integrity. Otherwise this society will rot from the inside.

Gift of Self

Vowed religious promise celibate chastity as a living statement of their total gift of self to God and to God's people. For those who truly have this call, it is a supreme act of agape—unselfish love. Granted, the road of celibate chastity represents a remarkable—and out of the ordinary—commitment. It is not the usual roadway in life. The vast majority of good-willed people serve God and God's people splendidly without a commitment to celibacy. At the same time, psychotherapist A. W. Richard Sipes, who has studied the question for several decades, calls those people who live out a true vocation to celibate chastity "awesome." What he goes on to say about these men—his study centered exclusively on Catholic priests—is quite wonderful and rings true: "They have successfully negotiated each step of celibate development at the more or less appropriate stage and are characterologically so firmly established that their state is, for all intents and purposes, irreversible. These truly are the eunuchs of whom Christ spoke in the New Testament (Matthew 19:12). . . . They manifest an interior freedom and integration that unite their individuality and their service. Their spirituality is marked by their efforts and achievements. In this group I witnessed the integrative and transformative power of the celibate reality. . . . Regularly I was struck by the practical effects and manifestations these men demonstrate in the most casual and natural way. Sexual integration rests easily on their shoulders because they have faced their inner sexual structure so thoroughly; gender, orientation, sexual desire have been confronted, penetrated and absorbed in the loneliness of a spiritual realm and perception of spiritual reality. . . . Celibate men led me to reconsider scripture; through them I gained an appreciation for the origins of celibate love and an understanding of St. Paul. They convinced me that the core of Christian and celibate experience was in St. Paul's exclamation, 'There is no longer Jew or Greek, slave or free, male or female; we are all one in Jesus Christ' (Galatians 3:29). . . . These male celibates are not afraid of sex; they are not competitive with married Christians; they do not fear or disdain women; they do not confuse celibacy with power or domination. Celibacy is their deeply personal, hard-won adjustment—they own it: it is their spiritual tie to the Reality most of them call God. These men are rare and a precious spiritual resource."[4]

These words obviously apply to vowed women as well. All of us have known religious sisters who live active and enormously productive lives, loving widely and well and finding total fulfillment in their unique vocation. In Sipes's words, "they are a rare and precious resource." These chaste celibates have truly given themselves.

A Social Commitment

Just like poverty, chastity is a prophetic social statement. Personally, I find this particular rationale for living with integrity in sexual matters especially compelling. For a variety of reasons—the pampered affluence of life in developed countries, a mentality that anything is OK as long as it doesn't hurt anybody, and an almost knee-jerk reaction to the prudishness about sex we had for so long—our culture has lost a sense of the God-given creative potential of genital sexuality and the reverence we ought to have in using it. A look at magazine racks in an average supermarket, a quick click through TV channels on any given day, and the explicitly erotic scenes in many current movies point to a culture that has pretty much gone insane about sex.

A few years ago I underwent an outpatient medical procedure and spent several hours recuperating in a small cubicle provided for that purpose. There were several of us going through the same process, and each of our curtained-off spaces had a small television set for our entertainment. In the cubicle right next to me was an older gentleman, whose wife and daughter were keeping him company, and I couldn't help overhearing their comments about the TV program they were watching.

It was one of those voyeuristic daytime shows (the word *show* is so apt—as in *showoff*) where the "guests" share with the host and the rest of the world incredibly intimate aspects of their lives. This particular program featured a young woman who made her living through prostitution and whose mother had no idea of the daughter's activities. The producers had arranged for an on-camera encounter between the two women, during which the daughter would "tell all." I could tell that my neighbors were really getting into the suspense that the host built up as he quizzed the young woman about the life she was living, about her relationship with her mother, and about the feelings she was having about revealing this secret. Judging from the comments they made, this middle-American family next to me was absolutely absorbed by the whole sick program.

What is worse, like the young woman on the program just described, it too often happens today that women in particular are used and manipulated for sexual entertainment. Typically, it's the female body that is suggestively depicted to promote that idol of our culture, sexual freedom, and in the ever-present advertisements that push products guaranteed to take away pain or to make us rich, powerful, or happy. We've gone beyond the bounds of a healthy appreciation for the beauty of women's bodies and the wonder of sexual relations and procreation they represent.

What can possibly bring our culture back to some sanity here if not a counter-culture committed to chastity, vowed or not? We're in desperate need of healthy women and men whose lives and actions make the case that giving free rein to genital sexuality brings anything but fulfillment in life—that, in fact, one sure way to happiness lies in respect and control of oneself with others in the area of sexuality. Chastity and celibacy are prophetic challenges to a world that has lost its sexual compass.

A Sign of God's Reign

Finally, chastity and celibacy also point to the in-breaking of God's reign in human history. Notice that I use the two words *chastity* and *celibacy* here. The two are not the same. Everyone is called to chastity; some are called to celibate chastity.

Persons who live with respect and integrity regarding their sexuality and that of every other person are witnesses to that future when God will bring about "the new heavens and the new earth" (Rv 21). They witness to what Jesus meant when he told the cynical religious leaders of his time that "when people rise from the dead, they neither marry nor are given in marriage" (Mt 22:30)—the fullness of the divine dream for humanity where God will be All in all. This rationale for chastity and celibacy will surely strike many as too otherworldly, too far away from our here-and-now experience. But, having a deepened understanding of Jesus' central message, God's reign on earth, helps us see why all spirituality must move us to engage with efforts to improve human life. And certainly, today, too many human lives are diminished and eventually crippled because of disrespect for sexuality.

It's probably true to say that very few people are paying much attention to these various reasons for chastity and celibacy, that today hardly anyone cares if people are chaste or not. We can even say that a culture like ours often scoffs at those who view sexuality seriously and act carefully. If this is true, then isn't it all the more reason for living with sexual integrity? Prophets typically are not heard in their own time and place, and chastity today is clearly the work of prophets. The challenge to live an engaged spirituality surely includes at our time and place in history speaking and acting on the truth about God's inestimable gift of sex and procreation in a world that has pretty much forgotten what a sacred trust that gift is.

Conclusion

A final word about poverty and chastity. As we live with all of the questions and circumstances, the choices and nuances that surround these ideals, we come face to face with our weaknesses and vulnerabilities. A consumer society and a culture of unbridled sexual activity bombard us on all sides. The so-called developed world, with the United States as its exemplar and driving force, pulls us continually to surround ourselves with "stuff," to pamper our bodies, to replace needs with wants, and to give in to every whim. It is enormously difficult to practice countercultural values like poverty and chastity in an environment like ours. We know only too well our flaws and missteps and failings as we move through life in the heart of the empire. In the face of all of this St. Paul has words of consolation and encouragement. They come from his second letter to the early Christian community at Corinth, a city that was also quite cosmopolitan and surely filled with the same kind of attractions that can divert and distract even very good-willed people today. In this part of his letter Paul is speaking about faith, but we can apply his words just as well to our struggles around the ideals of poverty and chastity: "This treasure we possess in earthen vessels, to make it clear that its surpassing power comes from God and not from us. We are afflicted in every way possible, but we are not crushed; full of doubts, we never despair. We are persecuted but never abandoned; we are struck down but never destroyed. Continually we carry about in our bodies the dying of Jesus, so that in our bodies the life of Jesus may also be revealed" (2 Cor 4:7–10).

Chapter 7

The Church and the New Creation

In August 1968, almost three years after the close of the Second Vatican Council, representatives from every Catholic Bishops' Conference of Central and South America met in Medellín, Colombia, to apply the vision and directives of the council to their world. What came out of that conference was a series of revolutionary documents that took a fresh look at every aspect of Latin American life and offered new pastoral responses to each situation. *The Church in the Present-Day Transformation of Latin America in the Light of the Council* described the reality of the church and society: "The traditionalists or conservatives show little or no social conscience, have a middle-class orientation and consequently do not question the social structures. In general they are primarily concerned with preserving their privileges which they identify with the 'established order'" (no. 6). And, "We ought to sharpen the awareness of our duty of solidarity with the poor, to which charity leads us. This solidarity means that we make ours their problems and their struggles, that we know how to speak with them" (no. 10). And also, "The Church sees in youth the constant renewal of the life of humanity. . . . Youth is a symbol of the Church, called to a constant renovation and renewal, that is, to a continual 'rejuvenation'" (nos. 10, 12).

Incredibly, these were bishops speaking, and they made it clear that the institutional church in Central and South America was making a conscious and historic choice. It was moving to situate the whole church—the People of God in Latin America—at the service of the poorest sectors of that society. That choice by the bishops was somewhat out of character for a group of hierarchs; it was a sea change for the powerful but top-heavy church institution in Latin America, and it turned out to have incredibly far-reaching effects. Let's play that out for a moment.

Turning away from centuries-old alignments with a feudal status quo, imposed and held in place by political and military power and the aristocratic elites, the church called itself to a preferential option for the poor (a phrase not actually found in the Medellín documents, but one that quickly became shorthand for their underlying spirit). From a church that had forever borrowed its theology and spirituality from other places, particularly from Spain, Medellín propelled the "liberationist" insights that became Latin America's unique gift to the universal church. In a community of faith that had always imported pastoral ministers in huge numbers from Europe and North America, this historical turnabout at Medellín inspired homegrown lay, religious, and clerical vocations. And predictably, what happened through the bishops at the Medellín conference sparked reprisals from the power elites whose vested interests had suddenly come under intense scrutiny and criticism. Within ten years of that 1968 Pentecost moment, fully a thousand pastoral ministers—mostly lay catechists—had been killed for the "crime" of preaching and living the preferential option for the poor.

For me, as a parish priest in Lima, Peru, at the time, it was a life-changing experience to feel the impact of the Medellín conference almost as soon as it finished its work. Because the great theologian of Medellín, Father Gustavo Gutiérrez, and one of its chief architects, Cardinal Juan Landazuri, both came out of the Peruvian church, we immediately got firsthand and stirring insights into what the church was calling for. Much of that story is detailed in *Birth of a Church,* my account of the upper-middle-class parish where I served in those days and which was utterly changed by Medellín.[1]

As a person of faith and a "cradle Catholic," I found my whole idea of spirituality pretty much turned upside down. With demands like the preferential option for the poor, the Latin American church helped me to see with new eyes what Jesus meant when he said that all of us will be judged exclusively on what we did or did not do for the "least of the brothers and sisters," and how complex the goal of nonviolence becomes in the light of the bishops' diagnosis that the Latin American reality was "institutionalized violence." Social sin came into my field of vision for the first time, as did social grace. And above all, I slowly came to understand the privileged place of the poor in salvation history— that God has a preferential option for the poor. Amazing stuff, which stretched and pushed and dragged me into a whole new way of looking at life's ultimate questions: Why are we here? Where are we going? What is the pathway?

What happened at Medellín was that the bishops of Latin America, unexpectedly and almost unbelievably, chose the reign of God, God's kingdom, the New Creation over their own ecclesiastical status, indeed over the church's security. With remarkable courage those bishops rolled the dice in favor of kingdom values, risking the historical power and prestige that the institutional church enjoyed in that part of the world. A conversion like that had to have been the work of the Holy Spirit; nothing else explains it.

Church and Reign

That great turnabout in the Latin American church helps us focus on the two overarching realities of the Christian's life in God—the church and the New Creation.[2] Any valid Catholic-Christian spirituality has to deal with both realities. The church claims to be the community that Jesus left behind to continue his work in the world; the New Creation was the principal theme of Jesus' teaching. So the church's main work is to help create space for the kind of spirituality that takes seriously the two great commandments—love of God and love of neighbor—in this historic moment. What is more, the promise and hope held out by the vision of God's New Creation make for a healthy, purposeful, and productive spirituality. Building God's reign on earth gives meaning to church life. Of course, the opposite is true as well, and tragically, not uncommon. When the church fails to put itself clearly at the service of the New Creation, the result is frustrating and often scandalous. All we have to do is compare the spirituality of people like Sister Dorothy Stang, martyred Brazilian missioner, with the "spirituality" of those who go around check-ing on minuscule liturgical rubrics these days.

Most of us American Catholic-Christians grew up with the church. In some places the local parish was our way of identify-ing our neighborhood roots: "I'm from St. Ambrose"; "I belong to St. Theresa's." We knew the parish had a pastor, with his priest associates and the sisters, who were usually connected with the parochial school. The rest of us were lay people, and we belonged to the parish, mostly, as the old saying goes, as praying, paying, and obeying members. It was all very neat and tidy, if top heavy. We learned that clusters of these parish struc-tures were stitched together into a diocese, with a bishop in charge. We became aware that all the dioceses of the world an-swered to a place called the Vatican, whose top official was the pope. So we came to know the church as a highly structured, tightly administered organization in which everyone was sup-posed to know his or her place. (A friend of mine once told me that as a boy of nine or ten he listened as the new pastor intro-duced himself to the parish with the words, "Every ship has a captain, and I'm captain of this ship.")

With the Second Vatican Council the notion of church as in-stitution was enlarged and expanded. One of the great documents of Vatican II, the *Dogmatic Constitution on the Church,* used an entire chapter to explain the church as the People of God. That new way of looking at the church brought out the reality of the church as community, where things were much more flexible. Who belonged to the community, who did not, and why—these were no longer as clear cut. In the decades since the Second Vatican Council lots of people have participated actively in the life and mission of the People of God without necessarily mak-ing any formal commitment to the institution. We've also surely known individuals of other Christian traditions who strike us as quite "Catholic" in their outlook and actions, in their apprecia-tion for our sacramental system, or in the value they place on Catholic social teaching. Recently I met a woman who told me that she had refrained from joining the Catholic Church so as not to offend her father, who was an Episcopal priest. When she did finally come into full communion as a Catholic, her father's reaction was "why did it take you so long?" For him, she had been Catholic all along.

Theologian Avery Dulles, S.J., has set out two further understandings of church—as herald and as servant. As herald, the church announces "integral" salvation, the movement, as Paul VI in *On the Development of Peoples* puts it, from "conditions of life that are less human to those that are more human" (no. 21). And the church as herald should—but doesn't always—have the courage to denounce all that stands the way of that movement. The social teaching of the church is a clear example of this dimension of church. Social document after social document holds out a vision and the hope of total liberation for all people and at the same time condemns the personal and social sins that stand in the way of that ideal. But the documents are just part of the vocation of the church as herald. In every part of the world today we have witnesses in all kinds of church-based movements and organizations that denounce the sins of this "culture of death" and shout out the possibilities for a better way. In the United States, Americans began to see the arrogance and futility of our government's planned invasion and occupation of Iraq, and thousands of church members took to the streets with tens of thousands of others before this tragedy began and declared that this country was blundering its way into a quagmire.

The church has a splendid history of servanthood. We know all sorts of religious congregations, as well as lay societies that were founded precisely to take care of orphans, the elderly, and the sick. Schools for poor children, hospices where dying people find some comfort, soup kitchens and night shelters for street people—these and so many more examples of charity, which continue right to this moment, show a church that has always seen itself as servant to a hurting world. It's probably safe to say that this dimension of church has gone a long way to absolve it for its gross shortcomings in other areas of human life: "Her many sins are forgiven because she has loved much" (Lk 7:47).

Finally, in the Second Vatican Council's *Dogmatic Constitution on the Church (Lumen Gentium)* the church spoke of itself as "a kind of sacrament" (no. 1). This was really an amazing insight, a moment of real inspiration—and grace. To call itself sacrament meant that the church let go of the pretensions it had held for centuries to being "a perfect society." Now it was, modestly, an external sign that pointed to a reality infinitely greater than itself, namely, final salvation in the New Creation. The great German theologian of the twentieth century, Karl Rahner, S.J., remarked that historians five hundred years from now will point back to this breakthrough insight about the church as the unique and lasting contribution of Vatican II. Quite a claim.

Keeping the understanding of church as institution, community, herald, servant, and especially as sacrament in mind, another statement from the Second Vatican Council provides a segue to the second part of this chapter. The *Pastoral Constitution on the Church in the Modern World (Gaudium et Spes)* says: "While helping the world and receiving many benefits from it, the Church has a single intention: that God's kingdom may come, and that the salvation of the whole human race may come to pass" (no. 45).

So the bottom line for the church is that it is in service to the New Creation; that it is in business, so to speak, for that purpose alone; and that the church and New Creation are not the same. This, I believe, is what the Latin American bishops opted for at the Medellín Conference, when they put the whole church on the side of the impoverished multitudes of their world and turned their backs in theory and in practice on the church's own privilege and power. They declared in effect that the church is most authentic when it serves the New Creation, and the history of the Latin American church after Medellín bears this out. This view of church-for-the-New Creation has enormous consequences for every one of us who tries to live a spirituality within the community that is the Catholic-Christian church. In fact, that vocation is at the heart of this book.

As a postscript to this reflection on church, it's important to revisit the need for penitence, especially in one area of Catholic life in this country. The scandal of priestly sexual abuse and the subsequent coverups by bishops, which have made such a mockery of the ideals of the church helping to build the New Creation and terribly weakened our faith communities, cry out for an attitude of penitence, reparation, remorse. This is especially true for priests and bishops. The other sisters and brothers in our household of faith should expect nothing less of those of us who, while perhaps personally innocent of wrongdoing in this scandal, publicly represent a clergy and episcopacy that have done untold harm. We need to make frequent public and personal acts of contrition for the sins of our brothers.

That holds true as well for all the sins of our church. In addition to the clergy-and-bishop scandal, we have a great deal for which to ask God's mercy and pardon in failing to serve God's reign in the world: frequent silence from hierarchy and laity alike in the heart of an empire that needs to hear a prophetic voice for peace, justice, and care for the planet; our immense institutional wealth; the conspicuous consumption of so many clergy and laity. We are a flawed community, like every community in history, and we're all in this church together. A humble and healthy attitude of repentance strikes me as absolutely necessary so that we neither turn a blind eye to the church's failings nor leave it in frustration.

Finally, despite all of its—and our—failings and sins, the church at its best keeps on trying to live out that "single intention," that God-given vocation stated in the *Pastoral Constitution on the Church in the Modern World*: "that God's kingdom may come and that the salvation of the whole human race may come to pass" (no. 45). We are "hard wired" to do this task even though so often we fall short.

The New Creation

So what exactly is this kingdom that the church says is so important? How do we define it? Where do we see it? What are its contours? What would the New Creation look like? Where does it appear? And especially, what role does each of us play in bringing it about? If bringing about God's kingdom is the "single intention" of the church, how is it that we don't seem to pay much attention to these questions? When, for example, was the last time any of us heard a homily based on questions such as these?

Lack of focus on the reign of God is really curious because right from the beginning the central theme of Jesus' message and ministry was the reality of the New Creation, the kingdom of God, God's reign breaking in on human history. In fact, Jesus' "advance man," John the Baptizer, announced this fact loudly and clearly: "Reform your lives! The reign of God is at hand" (Mt 3:2). From the moment Jesus appeared on the scene he said the same things: "Reform your lives! The kingdom of God is at hand" (Mt 4:17). All through the three years of his public ministry the Lord continually uses New Creation language: "The kingdom of God us like unto, . . . " "The reign of God is within you . . . , " "To what can we compare the reign of God?" The theme fills the pages of the Gospels.

Let me try to outline here some directions I've found helpful in thinking about the whole rich area of the reign of God, the New Creation. For the most part these lines of thought come out of the transforming experience I have had as part of a church that dramatically has acted on the conviction that it has to be a servant of God's reign on earth. I came to see that getting a handle on what the reign was all about made a huge difference in forging an engaged spirituality.

A View from Scripture

Jesus' own words and actions give us a clearer sense of the shape and the contours of the New Creation, as well as the values and signs that mark its presence. Some examples: Once, Jesus curtly dismissed pious objections that his disciples were violating religious laws when they ate corn on the Sabbath. He said, "The Sabbath was made for humankind, not humankind for the Sabbath" (Mk 2:27). The *freedom* to be fully human and to do what fully human people need to do strikes me as the lesson Jesus teaches here, a hallmark of the New Creation in the midst of so many "unfreedoms" and enslavements in human relations both personal and social.

The opponents of Jesus were forever sniping at Jesus for spending time with tax collectors, prostitutes, and sinners. Once he answered their moralistic objections with a brusque, "I have come to call not the righteous but sinners" (Mk 2:17). That attitude signaled the high value Jesus put on *inclusivity* and *human dignity*—surely signs of the New Creation.

In Jesus' blueprint for following him, the classic Sermon on the Mount, he tells us to "strive first for the kingdom of God and God's justice" (Mt 6:33). Making sure that each human person has what is his or her due—in other words, *justice*—stands as another indicator of God's reign on earth.

On that special occasion when he sat at table for the last time with his friends, Jesus pointed to a very definite value of the New Creation: "Peace I leave with you, my peace I give to you" (Jn 14:27). *Peace* is a hallmark of the reign of God.

At the same meal the Lord prayed for the disciples there with him and for all those down through the centuries who would be his disciples, "that all may be one as you Father are in me and I in you" (Jn 17:21). A growing *unity* among peoples points to the coming of the New Creation.

Finally, and above all, Jesus summed up in one commandment what the reign of God is all about: "Love one another as I have loved you" (Jn 15:12). *Love* is an essential part of the kingdom.

These words and actions of Jesus, and other parts of scripture, demonstrate that when people walk in freedom, live with dignity, and base their personal and social relationships on justice, peace, and unity, and when love governs the lives of God's daughters and sons, we can be sure that "the kingdom of God is among us."

Two other Bible texts help round out this overview of what the reign of God looks like. One is from the Prophet Isaiah, and the other from Revelation, and they are remarkably similar. They hold out a beautiful vision of the fullness of God's dream for humanity: "For I am about to create new heavens and a new earth; the former things shall not be remembered or come to mind. But be glad and rejoice forever in what I am creating; for I am about to create Jerusalem as a joy, and its people as a delight. I will rejoice in Jerusalem and delight in my people; no more shall the sound of weeping be heard in it, or the cry of distress. No more shall there be in it an infant that lives but a few days, or an old person who does not live out a lifetime; for one who dies at a hundred years will be considered a youth, and one who falls short of a hundred will be considered accursed. They shall build houses and inhabit them; they shall plant vineyards and eat their fruit. They shall not build and another inhabit; they shall not plant and another eat; for like the days of a tree shall the days of my people be, and my chosen shall long enjoy the work of their hands. They shall not labor in vain, or bear children for calamity; for they shall be offspring blessed by the Lord—and their descendants as well. Before they call I will answer, while they are yet speaking I will hear. The wolf and the lamb shall feed together, the lion shall eat straw like the ox; but the serpent—its food will be dust! They shall not hurt or destroy on all my holy mountain, says the Lord" (Is 65:17–25).

And from Revelation: "Then I saw a new heaven and a new earth; for the first heaven and the first earth had passed away, and the sea was no more. And I saw the holy city, the new Jerusalem, coming down out of heaven from God, prepared as a bride adorned for her husband. And I heard a loud voice from the throne saying, 'See, the home of God is among mortals. He will dwell with them as their God; they will be his peoples, and God himself will be with them; he will wipe every tear from their eyes. Death will be no more; mourning and crying and pain will be no more, for the first things have passed away.' And the one who was seated on the throne said, 'See, I am making all things new'" (Rv 21:1–5).

A View from Liturgical Language and Practice

There is a lot of kingdom imagery in liturgical practices of the Catholic-Christianity that reflects and reinforces the dream of a New Creation in human history and humanity's part in it. One is so very familiar that it can easily escape our attention: "thy kingdom come, thy will be done on earth as it is in heaven." But doesn't the fact that Jesus himself gave us those words and that plea have incredible significance both in terms of God's reign approaching and humanity's part in its arrival?

At every Catholic Eucharist, just before the Communion, the presider speaks a prayer in the name of the people assembled there, people "who wait in joyful hope for the coming of our Savior Jesus Christ." This prayer is all about "the day of the

Lord," the final in-breaking of the New Creation in human history.

The Fourth Eucharistic Prayer has these words: "He [Jesus] sent the Spirit from you, Father, as his first gift to those who would believe, so that *we might complete his work on earth* and bring ourselves and all people the fullness of your life." Completing Jesus' work on earth must refer to the final in-breaking of God's reign in human history.

We're always hearing public prayers in our Catholic-Christian tradition end with references to God's reign: "We make our prayer through Jesus Christ who with you and the Spirit lives and reigns world without end." The Lord's Prayer concludes this way: "For the kingdom, the power and the glory are yours now and forever, Amen."

The Preface of the Mass for the Feast of Christ the King has a kind of overview and hymn of praise to God for this compelling vision and goal of human existence—bringing about the New Creation. The words are based on St. Paul's incredible insights into the place that the crucified and risen Christ holds in salvation history and in bringing about the New Creation: "All powerful and ever-living God, we do well always and everywhere to give you thanks. You anointed Jesus the Christ, your only-begotten One, with the oil of gladness as the eternal priest and first-born of the Universe. As priest he offered his life on the altar of the cross and redeemed the human race by this one perfect sacrifice of peace. As first-born he claims dominion over all creation, that he may present to you, almighty One, an eternal and universal reign: a reign of truth and life, a reign of holiness and grace, a reign of justice, love and peace. And so with all the choirs of angels in heaven we proclaim your glory and join in their unending hymn of praise: Holy, Holy, Holy."

God's Work—and Ours

What's truly remarkable is the fact that every person in the world plays a role in bringing closer—or postponing—the arrival of God's reign on earth. As martyred Archbishop Romero once said, God is the "master builder" of the New Creation, but amazingly, we can help it come more quickly or, tragically, hold it back. Good-willed people advance the day when God's reign breaks into history by living out and working in behalf of the values that embody the New Creation. By the same token, actions and situations that go counter to those values postpone it.

A fairly obscure little observation in the Second Letter of Peter has always sort of jumped off the page at me in this regard. The apostle is writing to early Christians about the kind of people Jesus' followers ought to be: "holy in your conduct and devotion." Then he says an amazing thing: "[You ought to be] looking for the coming of the day of God, *and trying to hasten it!*" (2 Pt 3:11–12, emphasis added). To me, this says that we are "co-creators" with the Creator, trying to hurry along the "day of God," this divine project that is God's reign. In the same way that the Second Vatican Council pointed to the church's "one single intention," I believe that humanity too has the same "single intention"—trying to hasten the day of the Lord. What better vision is there around which to build a spirituality?

Consequences for the People of God

With the reign of God as the ultimate project of history, the church as an institution and a community of believers is never more authentic and relevant than when it is involved in promoting ("hastening") the New Creation. This was clearly the case with the Latin American church when it made its historic turn-around at the post–Vatican II Medellín conference and called itself to a preferential option for the oppressed majorities there. Before long, a vigorous theology of God's reign exploded in Latin America. Base communities working for the New Creation sprang up by the thousands in most countries of Latin America; lay, religious, and priestly pastoral service was seen by young people as a meaningful option. I remember right after Medellín church leaders in Lima began to teach summer courses to unpack the enormous implications of that conference for pastoral work. Before long, it was hard to find room for all the people, especially young people, who wanted to attend. Before ten years had elapsed after that conference, fully one thousand church people in Latin America who were working to implement that vision had been killed at the hands of those who preferred the status quo. In a few short years a once dormant church became relevant to every sector of Latin American life—all because it got totally engaged in the serious business of building God's reign.

The Track Record of the Catholic Church Here

We had an all-too-brief moment like this in the United States church as well. In 1983 the bishops of our country issued the pastoral letter *The Challenge of Peace: God's Promise and Our Response.* In it they took on the U.S. government's policies regarding nuclear weapons: "We do not perceive any situation in which the deliberate initiation of nuclear warfare on however restricted scale can be morally justified." The bishops did not do so well when they got into the matter of using of nuclear weapons as deterrents: "We have arrived at a strictly conditional moral acceptance of [nuclear] deterrence." Still, they got the attention of policymakers in this country because they were addressing real issues.

One morning as the bishops filed into a meeting called to finalize this peace pastoral, each of them found on his desk a copy of a letter from the national security advisor of the Reagan White House asking him to change the critical remarks about our nation's nuclear policies. To their credit the bishops did not back down an inch from their outspoken statements. That was a sort of "Medellín moment" in our U.S. church. By taking up urgent New Creation questions related to peace and threats to peace, the institutional church here took a stand on the side of vulnerable people against the empire that safeguards its position in the world by means of an ever-growing military establishment.

Three years later the U.S. bishops wrote another pastoral letter, *Economic Justice for All.* Again their tone reflected a preferential option for the poor: "Decisions must be judged in light of what they do for the poor, what they do to the poor, and what they enable the poor to do for themselves" (no. 24). This second pastoral did not raise the hackles of powerful people as the peace pastoral had done. Still, in hindsight these two documents represent a peak moment in the history of the church in the heart of the empire, and one that many of us would love to see come again. Because, tragically, in the last few years what we have heard is pretty much dead silence from the institutional church in the United States on so many urgent New Creation issues—and this at a time when U.S. society desperately needs a moral voice about where this empire is headed.[3] Except for continuous calls to end abortion, stem-cell research, and same-sex marriage—all legitimate issues—the church in our country has failed to condemn the war in Iraq (after meekly offering the opinion before 2003 that invading Iraq did not seem to square with the just-war theory), much less decry our government's warlike policies all across the globe. The church has said precious little recently about the growing divide between rich and poor, here and around the world. The church is mute on the obvious and growing threats to the environment. Where is the evidence of the "single intention"—that the kingdom of God come—in our official church today?

Conclusion–A Light at the End of the Tunnel

Since the Second Vatican Council proclaimed it, just about all of us in the Catholic community have gladly taken to heart that we are the church. It's part of our normal vocabulary. So the tasks that help realize God's dream for humanity and for the whole cosmos have to be our business, our tasks. That "single intention" that Vatican II spoke of has to be ours, not only the institution's. All of us who are church are co-creators of the New Creation. And despite thunderous silence from the institution today, we do have thousands of faith-filled people who take this vocation seriously, who make a lot of noise about all of the obstacles in the way of God's reign on earth. They reflect a true kingdom spirituality.

When we take on the New Creation tasks, conflict and opposition follow pretty quickly. The powerful of this world don't easily embrace values like freedom, inclusivity, justice, and peace; in fact, they invariably strike out against these threats to their privilege. The people in Latin America who accepted and acted on the vision of church expressed in the Medellín documents found this out very quickly. So does everyone else who begins to touch on the "anti-values" of people who are profiting by the injustices of the empire. Jesus spoke some words about situations like this that ought to encourage us to keep on speaking out for New Creation values and against whatever stands in their way: "My mission is to spread, not peace, but division" (Mt 10:34). "When they bring you before synagogues, rulers and authorities, do not worry about how to defend yourselves or what to say. The Holy Spirit will teach you at that moment all that should be said" (Lk 12:11–12).

A few years ago I saw all of this at work when I was part of a group invited to dialogue with officials from the International Monetary Fund (IMF) in Washington DC about our public criticisms of that institution's effectiveness in reducing world poverty. In his prepared statement the managing director of the IMF patronizingly lectured us about "the stern laws of the marketplace," making the point that those laws had to be observed and that if we understood more about such things, our criticisms of IMF policy would be more muted. One of our number took up the challenge and answered the director: "There are other stern laws as well: those cited by all the prophets, laws that judge institutions and societies on how they treat the widows, orphans, and strangers." That reply was perfect. While not in any way denying the "laws of the marketplace," our colleague appealed to a higher law. It was a New Creation statement, and as Jesus had predicted it was all that needed to be said that day. These are the kinds of testimonies we need constantly from a church community called to be at the service of God's reign in the midst of the empire today.

Chapter 8

• • • • •

Ecology

A few years ago some women religious asked me to preach a retreat at their motherhouse on issues of ecology and the sort of spirituality we need in dealing with them. I told the sisters that there were probably a hundred people who could treat this subject better than I could, but that I'd take a crack at it if they would agree to a sort of dialogue retreat. So we went at it.

The first evening I posed two hypotheses: first, that poor people are the first ones to feel the effects of polluted air, water, and soil; and, second, that there's a strong connection between ecology and our Catholic sacramental system. At that point I was surprised to hear a ripple of laughter go through the audience. I hadn't thought that the two proposals were particularly funny, so afterward I asked one of the sisters what the laughter was all about. She told me that a short time before they had invited a world-famous ecologist, also a Catholic priest, to give a series of lectures. Toward the end of his time with them, the sisters asked the same questions I had posed: Aren't the poor the first witnesses to violations of the environment? Isn't there a connection between ecology and the sacraments? The priest's answer was curious: "I don't deal in those kinds of reflections." The sisters found it really amusing that without any specialized background in the field of ecology, I had started off our discussions with the very questions dismissed by the "expert."

That anecdote says a lot, I believe, about the need for more attention to ecology in working at a spirituality relevant to our times and our place in the world. It's fine to have scientific knowledge about things like global warming and the future of the planet, but what about these issues for people of faith living in the United States? Awareness of the grave dangers that face our beautiful but fragile natural environment and the effects those dangers are having, especially on the poor, brings with it an urgency about ecological justice. These are not just academic, theoretical questions but moral and theological matters as well. And because our country plays a huge part in both their causes and possible solutions, any engaged spirituality *has* to come to grips with ecological issues. I'm convinced that the twenty-first century will see much, much more work done by spiritual writers on the connections between the Christian view of creation and all the pressing challenges facing our environmental home today. This next frontier cries out for attention.

The topic, of course, is vast. Even a partial listing of the issues that environmentalists and increasing numbers of ordinary folks worry about today gives a clue to the breadth and depth of the problem and to the immense task ahead in working out a spirituality that informs and inspires individuals and whole societies to tread respectfully on the earth and to care for all of creation:

1. Seventy-three mammal species have become extinct, and one of those left is in decline due to uncontrolled logging, new roads, hunting for food, skins and the pet trade (U.N. Food and Agriculture Organization report, 2000).
2. During the 1990s, 9.4 million hectares of forest (roughly the land area of Portugal) were lost yearly (U.N. Food and Agriculture Organization report, 2000).
3. According to the World Meteorological Organization, 2003 was the third warmest in 150 years. Since 1990 we have experienced the ten warmest years on record with global carbon emissions (from fuel use) amounting to seven billion tons in 2003, up from two billion tons in 1950. The United States contributes nearly 25 percent to this pollution (United Nations, U.S. Department of Energy, and International Energy Agency reports, 2005). According to the World Watch Institute, energy demand will grow by 54 percent by 2025.
4. The average land-ocean temperature at the earth's surface went from 13.8 celsius in 1880 to 14.6 celsius in 2005—but

the rate of change has tripled since 1976. If this trend continues, an estimated 18 percent to an astounding 35 percent of the world's species will be gone by 2050 ("State of the World 2005," World Watch Institute).

5. Temperatures in the Arctic have risen at a rate almost double the worldwide average. And ice coverage has decreased by 15-20 percent over the past thirty years ("Vital Signs—2005," World Watch Institute).

6. The World Bank in 2000 projected that an average of 1.8 million people will die prematurely each year between 2001 and 2020 due to air pollution.

7. According to the Environmental Protection Agency, reductions in ozone levels will lead to higher levels of ultraviolet light. Laboratory and epidemiological studies demonstrate that ultraviolet light causes non-melanoma skin cancer and plays a major role in malignant melanoma development.

8. Five percent of the world's population (the United States) is responsible for nearly 25 percent of global carbon emissions ("Vital Signs—2005," World Watch Institute).

9. It seems clear to me, as well, that ominous possibilities surround indiscriminate genetic manipulation, unexamined development of new forms of plant and animal life, and experimentation regarding the origins of human life itself.

After listing areas of concern in the world, such as demographic imbalances, the spread of infectious diseases, growing human pressure on natural resources like land and oil, Christopher Flavin, president of the World Watch Institute, wrote in late 2004: "The possibility of disruptive climate change may be an even greater threat to the security of societies. Amid new signs of accelerated global warming . . . scientists are focusing on the potential for the sudden collapse of economically essential ecosystems, such as forests, underground water resources and coastal wetlands. The unprecedented four hurricanes that devastated Florida in 2004 (pre-Katrina), combined with the record number of typhoons that hit Japan (pre-tsunami), left weather forecasters studying the possibility that catastrophic weather events could soon become the norm—with immense human consequences, particularly in the world's poorest countries."

Toward a Spirituality of Ecology

In the early days of liberation theology in Latin America, before it even *had* a name, it was common for those of us who were there to receive copies of essays from people like Father Gustavo Gutiérrez with titles like "Toward a View from the Underside of History" or "Lines of Thought about the Privileged Place of the Poor in Salvation History." That's the kind of initial and tentative probing I am aiming at here.

It's clear that a single chapter on the spiritual dimensions of ecology cannot possibly do justice to the topic. I simply want to offer here some directions that might help integrate into a relevant and engaged spirituality the various issues related to environmental justice. This growing spirituality of ecology will certainly be seen some day as another of those new graces in the church. Here let me simply put forward some basic lines for reflection, beginning with the word *ecology* itself and a working definition/description of it taken from Leonardo Boff's *Ecology and Liberation: A New Paradigm*.

In the nineteenth century a German biologist, Ernst Haeckel, coined the word *ecology*, which he took from two Greek words, *oikos* (house) and *logos* (reflection or study). So *ecology* literally means the "study of our house." According to Leonardo Boff, "Ecology has to do with the relations, interaction, and dialogue of all living creatures (whether alive or not) among themselves and with all that exists. This includes not only nature (natural ecology), but culture and society (human ecology, social ecology, and so on)."[1] Boff's prose always reminds me of concentrated orange juice—very dense and in need of diluting so that the rest of us can understand a bit better his profound thought. What I understand him to be saying in this description of ecology is that everything that exists is in relationship; nothing and no one exist outside of "relation, interaction, and dialogue."

That lovely thought takes us right to the core Christian belief that this earthly home of ours and indeed the entire cosmos come from the incredibly generous initiative of a loving Creator. When we review the different ways our faith tries to speak about God, the mind reels in thinking about creation. The One Who Is, with no beginning and no end, the totally perfect, eternal Trinity of truth and love, the One who is totally Other loved everything into being. God shared the divine life in creating other realities independent of that divine Self. Divine munificence, prodigality, gratuitousness caused God to fling a universe out and to sustain it for eons and eons. Our world is the work of the One who is Love, held in existence by divine will, and therefore sacred. Creation has immense intrinsic value in and of itself because it comes from God and continues to be sustained by God's power. This simple, basic, and profound fact inspires all the rest we might say about an ecological dimension of spirituality. In fact, the point has been made that God's first self-revelation is not the Bible but creation. When you think about that, it makes all kinds of sense. Creation is the first clue we have about God.

There are all sorts of ways to probe for further directions to a spirituality of ecology. I believe that in a book like this one a short review of the previous chapters will serve best. Each chapter is really a building block of Catholic-Christian spirituality, and they all dovetail neatly with our living in and caring for the physical world around us. Obviously a lot more could be said about each of the following categories and its relation to ecology. I'll leave it to the reader's imagination and creativity to push these reflections further.

Incarnation

The belief that God became human is fundamental to building an authentic Creation spirituality. The One who carried out the marvelous work of creation also touched our world intimately, personally, by actually becoming a part of it in the historical person Jesus of Nazareth. In our own flesh and bones God has walked on the land, breathed the air, and drunk the water, just like every other living thing. To believe that the Creator conjoined with creation brings us to a deeper sense of reverence for our planet and the whole cosmos.

During a trip to Israel about twenty years ago I remember arriving at Nazareth one afternoon, and as soon as our van stopped at the hospice where we were going to stay, feeling that

I needed to kneel down and kiss the ground. (The driver thought that I had taken sick and jumped out of the van to help me up.) But at that moment I had the powerful memory of Jesus, the incarnate Word of God, living in that town for around thirty years, running through those streets as a boy; looking out over the surrounding hills in his young manhood; setting out from there to join John the Baptizer at the Jordan River—for me Nazareth was sacred ground. The incarnation of God as one of us made that place (and all places) holy, and I felt it appropriate to kneel and reverence the land where Jesus had walked.

Belief in the amazing fact of God's becoming flesh gives ecology a perfect spiritual foundation.

A Political (Ecological) Reading of the Scriptures

After the insistence in Chapter 2 on a political reading of the scriptures, it follows naturally that we need to develop a similar ecological reading of God's word as well. And that shouldn't be so hard to do. The New Testament is filled with references to creation. Jesus used all sorts of earthy images in his teaching and ministry: farmers going out into the fields to sow grain; tiny mustard seeds as metaphors for God's reign; the fields ripe for the harvest. He told us to watch the lilies of the fields and the birds of the air and learn trust from them. He spoke about the need for us to read the signs of the times the same way that we read approaching changes in the weather. He calmed the wind and the waves. And he constantly broke bread with his friends, and that ordinary ritual became the gesture by which we would forever after recognize him. While God was with us he showed that he was in close touch with every element of the physical world around him.[2]

St. Paul always amazes me with his insights about the place and role of the Christ in regard to creation. He goes beyond where I would expect such an early follower of Jesus to be in terms of knowing the cosmic repercussions of God becoming human. For example, Paul calls Christ "the firstborn of all creation" and says that in Christ "all things in heaven and on earth were created" (Col 1:15–16). He speaks about Jesus' death and resurrection as an event that brought God and every created thing back together, that God was "pleased . . . through Christ to reconcile to himself all things, whether on earth or in heaven" (Col 1:19–20). This early apostle wrote that God has a plan "for the fullness of time to gather up all things in him [Christ], things in heaven and things on earth" (Eph 1:10). And in his letter to the Christians of Rome, Paul talks about the future of creation in phrases like these: "[It] will be set free from its bondage to decay and will obtain freedom . . . the whole creation [which] has been groaning in labor pains until now" (Rom 8:21–22). What far-reaching perceptions and inspirations about the destiny of our universe! And such rich food for thought about the awesomeness and connectedness of everything God has created!

The earlier Hebrew scriptures, too, constantly call attention to God's world, beginning, of course, with the stories of creation in Genesis, and how when the Creator looked at creation, it was "very good" (Gn 1:31). The great Jubilee ideal and the prophetic tradition that run through the scriptures have many references to living on one's own land and cultivating one's own crops and vines. And there are warnings about the consequences for the earth and its creatures that follow when people turn unfaithful and disloyal to God: "The land mourns, and all who live in it languish; together with the wild animals and the birds of the air, even the fish of the sea are perishing" (Hos 4:1–3).

God's revealed word is first of all an ecological word.

Prayer and Contemplation

It's a common experience to find inspiration for prayerful praise of God in the beauty of creation. The connection is, as we say, a "no brainer." To stand on the seashore and look at the vast, alive, powerful ocean; to drink in yet another spectacular sunset; to gaze at a giant tree or feel a cool breeze; even to find a brave little flower emerge from cracks in a concrete sidewalk on a city street—all of these remind us that God's creative activity and sustaining presence continue to grace the whole world. We've all had times when created beauty nearly overwhelmed us and breathless prayers of adoration and thanksgiving welled up in us.

I remember stopping my jeep on a remote mountain road in Bolivia one day just to immerse myself in the utter magnificence of my surroundings. The imposing Andean peaks rose all around me, snow covered and sun drenched. But in that absolutely gorgeous, awe-inspiring setting what most struck me was the utter, complete silence—and I felt the presence of God with enormous gratitude.

All of creation's gifts around us help us move through the world with a truly contemplative attitude, one that the lovely hymn "How Great Thou Art" puts into words:

> O Lord my God! When I in awesome wonder
>   consider all the worlds thy hands have
>   made,
> I see the stars, I hear the rolling thunder, thy
>   pow'r throughout the universe displayed,
> Then sings my soul, my Savior God to thee;
> How great thou art, how great thou art!

How can our beautiful natural environment not spark prayer and a contemplative mindset?

Sin and Grace

What a horror, then, to find out that this beautiful, welcoming home that humanity calls earth is being chewed up, spoiled, and wasted by some people's greed and indifference. Moreover, it's amazing to me that the leaders of the empire even look beyond this earthly home to outer space as a place from which to launch weapons against our "enemies." By what right do they appropriate creation for their own self-serving ends? Who gives anyone permission to consume too much and to pollute air, water, and soil, which have been created and then personally touched by God, which have been given freely by the Creator for our respectful use, and which are so finite? And how dare we step outside of our earthly environment and look for ways to deploy military arms in the heavens so that we can better control this planet! Do we think we are gods with the power to destroy the world in a nuclear holocaust? This kind of arrogance is pure blasphemy, sin writ large.

Speaking from a totally different consciousness, Francis of Assisi praised the Creator for "brother sun, sister moon, mother earth, sister water, brother fire." What I think is enormously important in this Franciscan understanding of creation is that nothing, certainly not human beings, stands outside of the web of life. More and more people today know that we're all part of the environment and subject to its laws and limits. That growing awareness is helping us to walk more gently on the earth, to use God's gifts carefully and sparingly, and to resist as much as we can every aspect of the empire's presumptuous domination. Today, more and more efforts go to reversing depleted ozone layers, addressing global warming, recovering vast deforested and desertified areas, and challenging the thoughtless tinkering with the very building blocks of life. These are actions inspired by grace.

Once again, just as in every other area of life, sin and grace operate side by side in the way human beings act toward the environment.

Obedience

If it's true that creation, rather than scripture, is God's first self-revelation, then it must be that the Holy Spirit basically guides us through the laws of nature. When we pay attention to the physical world around us and listen attentively to our own bodies, we get clear indications of where obedience to God's loving Spirit is leading us in caring for creation. On the other hand, we disobey these guidelines at our own peril. Nature does not forgive; there comes a limit beyond which the harm will be irreparable. Whole species of plants and animals have disappeared forever because we polluted their habitats; rainforests have been sacrificed to thoughtless logging enterprises; rivers and lakes have died because we dumped tons of sludge into them. This cannot be the will of the Holy Spirit. Our God-given vocation includes obedience to and stewardship of the natural order. We are members of the community of all life.

Poverty and Chastity

Building up in ourselves a spirit of poverty can go a long way to helping us walk gently, respectfully, and sparingly on the earth. There is no need to hoard the Creator's gifts. God is a God of enough—for all. Poverty of spirit tells us we must live in ways that recognize that resources are finite, that others have as much right to them as we do, that might does not make right, that our planet is in danger—and living this way brings the kind of happiness that comes from a sense of contentment and integration. I have to say from my own experience of trying to live a healthy spirit of poverty in sparse and even austere surroundings (Bolivia, Peru, inner-city Washington DC), flawed and limited as that experience is, has brought me peace at the core of my being. Much more important, in the midst of a finite and fragile natural environment a habit of poverty is a gift to our endangered planet.

Chaste care and respect for our own beautiful bodies and those of everyone around us help us be aware that we are special creations of a loving God made in that God's very image and likeness. We present ourselves to the physical world and move in it through our bodies; they are dwelling places of the Divine, lent to us for the time of our sojourn on this earth. The care and respect we owe our bodies stretches from loving concern for our own physical well-being, our emotional balance, and our mental health all the way to integrity in the way we share our most intimate selves with other persons and finally to the sacred possibility of bringing about new life within the covenant of "two in one flesh." This consciousness takes us seamlessly to a deep respect for every organism around us. Chastity is a towering environmental issue when we see our physical beings as part of God's wonderful creation.

The Church and God's Reign

The church, the People of God, would not fulfill its vocation as a sacrament of salvation if it showed little concern for the creation and the threats that face it. The quotations from St. Paul above show us something of God's plan for creation, that the whole cosmos is moving toward some kind of final resolution that is bound up with salvation: "[Creation] will be set free from its bondage to decay and will obtain freedom" (Rom 8). So as humanity gradually comes to see the unity of everything in creation and how relatively easy it is to shatter that unity, Catholic social teaching has begun to address these things. Lots more on ecology will have to come from the Catholic-Christian tradition, and surely the next decades will see far greater attention paid to it by theologians, ethicists, and teachers in our faith community. But we have made a start. As early as 1963, Pope John XXIII in *Peace on Earth* spoke about threats to the earth, pointing out that nuclear testing could "lead to serious danger for various forms of life on earth" (no. 111). Paul VI, in his message to the Stockholm Conference on Human Environment, June 1, 1972, stated that "our generation must energetically accept the challenge of going beyond partial and mediate aims to prepare a hospitable earth for future generations."

Several times John Paul II took up concern for ecology. In his 1987 encyclical *The Social Concerns of the Church (Solicitudo Rei Socialis)*, for example, he includes ecology among the issues that must concern us today: "It is evident that development, the planning which governs it, and the way in which resources are used must include respect for moral demands. One of the latter undoubtedly imposes limits on the use of the natural world. The dominion granted to man by the Creator is not an absolute power, nor can one speak of a freedom to 'use and misuse,' or to dispose of things as one pleases. The limitation imposed from the beginning by the Creator himself and expressed symbolically by the prohibition not to 'eat of the fruit of the tree' (cf. Genesis 2:16–17) shows clearly enough that, when it comes to the natural world, we are subject not only to biological laws but also to moral ones, which cannot be violated with impunity" (no. 34).

In his address to the United Nations, August 18, 1985, John Paul II spoke about the stewardship that we need to exercise, taking into account "the needs of future generations." He got more specific in 1994, when he wrote in his apostolic letter "Tertio Milennio Adveniente" about the approaching millennium year:

"A more careful control of possible consequences on the natural environment is required in the wake of industrialization, especially in regard to toxic residue, and in those areas marked by an excessive use of chemicals in agriculture."

Finally, in a hard-hitting portion of his January 2001 general address, Pope John Paul II listed the areas that "humiliate the earth, that flower-bed that is our dwelling. . . . Humanity has disappointed the divine expectation. Above all in our time, man has unhesitatingly devastated wooded plains and valleys, polluted the waters, deformed the earth's habitat, made the air unbreathable, upset the hydrogeological and atmospheric systems, blighted green spaces [and] implemented uncontrolled forms of industrialization."

And now Pope Benedict XVI is continuing the thrust of his predecessors with regard to our duty to the environment. His words in an address given August 27, 2006, could have been directed to those of us who live in the empire: "The created world . . . is presently exposed to serious risks by life choices and lifestyles that can degrade it. . . . In particular, environmental degradation makes poor people's existence intolerable."

These are the cries of a church at the service of God's New Creation, a concern that obviously involves the natural order. The "new heavens and the new earth" of the Prophet Isaiah and the Book of Revelation are built on what God has brought into being. In addition, the values of the New Creation—freedom, dignity and inclusiveness, justice, peace, unity, and love—have to be reflected on and lived out in the context of the integrity of creation, with all of the threats to that lovely ideal today. This is an enormous "to do" list for our faith community living as we do at the center of a society and culture that moves in a very different direction.

Ecological concerns lie at the forefront of the church's service to God's reign.

Sacraments as Statements about Creation

The Catholic-Christian sacramental system is all about earthiness. Baptism with water symbolizes the cleansing, refreshing,

and yes, the dying and the rising that actually take place in the
baptized person. The oil used in confirmation recalls the calm-
ing and energizing gifts of the Holy Spirit that get us ready for
our responsibilities as mature followers of Christ. Breaking the
bread and sharing the cup of wine are the way Jesus wanted us
to remember him on our life's journey. The covenant of marriage
is not completed until sexual intercourse takes place. Ordination
to priestly service requires the physical touch of a bishop. Like-
wise, the sacrament of the sick uses touch and anointing the
same way Jesus so often supported and healed people who were
ill or traumatized. Every sacrament teaches over and over the
great lesson of Catholic Christianity—that everything touchable,
smellable, tasteable, everything sensual, is a gift from God. We'll
get many more rich insights into the connection between sacramental rituals and the natural world as people of faith continue
to think about our *oikos* (house) as part of their spirituality.

The sacraments are deeply ecological gestures.

Ecological Justice

Like every other dimension of spirituality, ecology goes beyond
any one person's or any particular group's right to a healthy environment. These matters are above all social questions because
they affect every society and all peoples on the planet. I believe
that ecological justice is just what a spirituality, which includes
ecology, has to aim at. This seems so obvious as not to need
elaboration. We can't have environmental movements that content themselves with cleaning up the air, water, and soil only for
those who can afford it or for the ones who make the most noise
about these cleanups—privileged folks whose demands usually
get taken seriously. The hypothesis I posed at the beginning of
this chapter continues to challenge everybody who takes a serious look at the state of the earth; that is, that poor people all over
the world are the first to feel ecological injustices—the pollution
of air, water, and soil—and to feel them worse than the rest of
us. I believe it's the poor who most urgently stand in need of everything that goes into ecological justice.

Yet, incredibly, concern about and action to clean up rivers and streams, to take away noxious air, and to get rid of toxic landfills often are initiatives of the powerful, *for* the powerful, confined to places where the powerful live. I saw this play out in two very different settings.

The first was in a dialogue some years ago sponsored by the influential Christian magazine *Sojourners.* The dialogue took place between two environmental experts, who came at these issues from very distinct perspectives. One was white and comfortably middle class, and his concerns about the integrity of the environment seemed to begin and end with himself and his limited world. The other was an African American who immediately began to speak about ecological justice, especially for people suffering because of bad water, polluted air, and depleted soil— all around the world. It wasn't surprising that the dialogue hoped for by *Sojourners* never got off the ground. It ended almost before it began, because there was no common ground between these two men and their outlook on the world. There was no way of bridging their different understandings of environmental issues, forged as each one was by his life experience.

I had another look at how hard it is to insert the idea of ecological justice into the debate on environmental health when I was working on weekends at a parish located in a Boston suburb called Woburn. I began to hear from the people that their community had lost an unusual number of its children to a fatal kind of leukemia. As the people tried to figure out what was going on, they found out that two local companies had a long history of dumping their toxic waste into the ground. Over time, it had leeched its way into the town's drinking water. There was a clear cause and effect between the polluted water and the blood disease that was killing the community's children in disproportionate numbers.

A best-selling book entitled *A Civil Action*—and later a movie based on the book—documented the only partially successful efforts of Woburn residents to bring the offending companies to justice. The book and the movie showed in detail the awful social costs that the actions of just two companies represented in the lives of an entire community—and the despicable efforts those companies made to avoid accountability. *A Civil Action* was a compelling case study about social sin and particularly about the urgent need for ecological justice.[3]

Conclusion

It won't surprise the reader when I bring to a close this admittedly introductory and incomplete reflection on ecology and spirituality with a much-quoted poem from St. Francis of Assisi about creation. It spans eight centuries but continues to hold wonderful insights for us today, as we begin again to appreciate God's self-revelation in nature. This beautiful "Canticle of Brother Sun" was written near the end of the saint's life. It was a time when he was experiencing terrible physical and emotional pain; he was nearly blind, wasted physically from a life of penance (which he himself finally saw as excessively harsh), and suffered all sorts of doubts and misgivings about the way the movement he had begun, the dream of his life, was being undercut and compromised by lesser men. Yet even in that diminished state this lover of God's creation could still find within himself the following words of praise:

> Most High, all-powerful, all good Lord!
> All praise is yours, all glory, all honor and
>   blessing.
> To you alone, Most High, do they belong.
> All praise be yours, my Lord, through all that
>   you have made,
> And first my Lord, Brother Sun,
> Who brings the day and light You give us
>   through him.
> How beautiful is he, how radiant in all his
>   splendor!
> Of you, most High, he bears the likeness.
>
> All praise be yours, my Lord, through Sister
>   Moon and Stars;
> In the heavens you have made them bright
>   and fair.

All praise be yours, my Lord, through
    Brothers Wind and Air,
And fair and stormy, all the weather's moods,
By which you cherish all that you have made.

All praise be yours, my Lord, through Sister
    Water,
So useful, lowly, precious and pure.

All praise be yours, my Lord through Brother
    Fire,
Through whom you brighten up the night.
How beautiful he is, how gay! Full of power
    and strength.

All praise be yours, my Lord, through Sister
    Earth, our mother,
Who feeds us in her sovereignty and produces
Various fruits and colored flowers and herbs.

All praise be yours, my Lord, through those
    who grant pardon
For love of you; through those who endure
    sickness and trial.
Happy those who endure in peace,
By you, Most High, they will be crowned.

All praise be yours, my Lord, through Sister
    Death,
From whose embrace no mortal can
    escape. . . .

Praise and bless my Lord and give thanks.
Serve God with great humility.

Francis's canticle shows why Pope John Paul II in November 1979 named him the patron of ecologists. The saint clearly had an understanding of himself and every other human being as a sister or brother in relationship with the entire created order. In his view we do not stand above or astride the earth and the cosmos; we are not here to dominate nature; we are a unique part of God's creation. That is an amazing insight for a person of the thirteenth century, or, for that matter, any century.

But it is not enough. Our task as the third millennium unfolds is ever so much more challenging. We have to deepen and broaden Francis' vision so that it stretches us to understand and engage with today's environmental realities, bringing to bear on the powers and principalities all of the insights and knowledge we have acquired, particularly in the last half-century, about our threatened natural habitat. This challenge is immensely important today, when the empire and giant corporations seem to take for granted that Mother Earth and even outer space are their playground, places where they can do whatever feeds into their bottom line—profit, power, and security.

We have a long, long way to travel on the way to ecological consciousness, respect, and justice. And there are incredible forces trying to block that road. Just think of the disregard our country has shown in recent years for the minimal requirements of the 2004 Kyoto Protocols regarding global warming. It's not in the empire's interests to respect the environment and earth's limited resources because the empire is founded and prospers precisely on their exploitation. In the end only an engaged spirituality that takes ecological justice seriously will be able to turn the tide away from that kind of destructive mentality. I think that only a deep and ever-widening spirituality that sees our earthly environment as sacred, fragile, defenseless, threatened, and ultimately our only home in the universe will give humanity the will to save it.

St. Francis's own words, also spoken in those dark and despondent days near the end of his life, say it all in this regard: "I have done what was mine to do. May Christ teach you what is yours."

Chapter 9

• • • • •

Eucharist

During the brutal dictatorship of Bolivian General Hugo Banzer in the 1970s, a group of poor, indigenous miners wound up in jail because of their political activities opposing the regime. Normally, one more violation of human rights in that country would have passed unnoticed—just one more case of blatant injustice against a few "faceless" Indians on the part of a repressive military government. However, this case was different. For some reason—call it desperation or foolhardiness or God's providence—the womenfolk of the incarcerated workers decided to protest the government's action and went on a hunger strike. Again, the action of a handful of Indian women—mothers, wives, sisters of some "no account" peasants—wouldn't normally have caused much of a stir there. Who would care if they starved themselves to death? But surprisingly, on this occasion the women's action took hold. People in the neighborhood, then the region, and soon around the country began to join the hunger strike or take to the streets and in a variety of creative ways demonstrated against this latest example of state terrorism in their country.

In seemingly record time the opposition became a national movement and began to spark international attention. Human rights groups in other countries knew that the Banzer government was perfectly capable of violently wiping out the growing opposition, so they called for observers from various countries to fly immediately to La Paz in a show of solidarity with the protestors. A representative from the U.S. Catholic Conference of Bishops volunteered to go and told the following story on his return some weeks later.

When Banzer's people took stock of the national and international crisis that faced them, they knew it was time for a strategic retreat. They gave in for the moment. The original several detainees were freed from jail, as were many others also being held as political prisoners. (As it turned out, this nonviolent, grass-roots protest soon led to the downfall of that dictatorship.) And the observer from the United States reported that when the women who had begun the protest heard the news that their men folk would return to them unharmed and that they could end their hunger strike, these poor, marginalized, unsophisticated Indians asked for holy communion as their first food.

Central Act of a Lived
Catholic-Christian Spirituality

In a moment we'll return to that wonderful story, but first a few words about Eucharist as the central action in any authentic Catholic-Christian—and engaged—spirituality. Everything in our tradition both comes out of and culminates in the "dangerous memory" of Jesus' death and resurrection, which we call to mind each time we celebrate the Lord's Supper. Even a quick review of developments in our awareness and practice of Eucharist over the past generation or so points to the fundamental place it holds in the Catholic-Christian's life with God—in our spirituality. Many will be familiar with these remarkable changes, but recalling them is a useful thing to do, especially at a time when a new generation of churchmen seems intent on rolling them back.

A lot of us still remember when the Mass and communion were very private, mysterious rites. We "heard" Mass, passively, in a foreign language, the priest standing with his back to us, the whole assembly kneeling in respectful silence. We went up to the altar rail for communion with our eyes down and returned to our place the same way for isolated prayer. In those days each person communed alone with Jesus, separated from the rest of the congregation, all of whom were doing the same.

We smile a little bit today at that individualistic, withdrawn, mystery-shrouded understanding of Eucharist. Nevertheless, Mass and communion in the "old days" were true acts of faith. They were moments of genuine prayer, and they expressed the conviction that endures to today: the Lord's Supper is a point of arrival and a point of departure for the People of God. Generations of holy, courageous, and exemplary Catholic-Christians—people like St. Thérèse of Lisieux, Blessed Pope John XXIII, and Dorothy Day, just to mention three—received nourishment and satisfaction from those older forms.

I remember as a boy observing my own father's attitude toward his once-a-month "communion Sunday." When I asked him why he did not receive the Eucharist more often, he said simply that he hadn't been brought up in the era of "frequent communion," as they called it then. But his approach to those special Sundays always impressed me: the sacrament of penance on Saturday evening, laying out his best clothes on Sunday morning, attendance at the earliest Mass, and, above all, his reverence when he actually received the host. He was not showy in his religious practices, but I knew that my father considered that once-a-month ritual very special, and I'm sure it helped me come to my own deep appreciation for the holy Eucharist. In my memory this was the best of the "old way."

With the Second Vatican Council came a new consciousness and a broader understanding of Eucharist in the Catholic-Christian world. In fact, aside from the essentials, we would hardly recognize ourselves today as the same faith community that half a century ago celebrated the Eucharist so differently. Now the accent is on communal rather than on individual participation in what is taking place at the altar, more on the meal (the Lord's Supper) than on the mystery (the Holy Sacrifice), and much more on our engagement in the action taking place than on passive attendance. With the prayers of the Mass now in local languages, the altar facing the people, and others besides the priest contributing to the celebration—in ministries of music, scriptural proclamation, commentaries, communion distribution—an entirely new and deeper appreciation for the wonder of this sacrament has taken over communities of faith. We are all the richer for this sea change.

What is more, the "worldly," here-and-now dimension of Eucharist has taken center stage. We offer to God the bread and the wine as "fruits of the earth and work of human hands"; we plead for all sorts of "secular" needs in our prayers of the faithful; we exchange signs of Christ's peace as citizens of a country and a world that so desperately need that peace; we hear our presiders pray for and about us as those who "wait in joyful hope for the coming of our Lord Jesus"; we find ourselves praying that "we might complete Jesus' work on earth and bring ourselves and others the fullness of grace." The ritual speaks not only about Eucharist as a point of arrival for the faith community, but its point of departure as well. "The liturgy is ended. Go in peace to love and serve."

A young married woman once spoke publicly about this outward and relational thrust of Eucharist when she went down the list of those she brought with her to the moment of offering at Mass. In the first place, she said, her husband and children were very much with her in thought, as well as her parents, brothers, sisters, and extended family; she said too that she offered to God friends and acquaintances, and even people whom she knew only casually; she also brought to mind all of the people living on earth today, and those that were once alive, and those who one day will live; finally, she explained, she offered to God the whole created universe: earth, planets, stars, the entire cosmos in grateful praise of the Creator. This woman had a remarkable modern understanding of the height, and breadth, and depth of Eucharist.

Eucharist as Subversive

The Eucharist is also a subversive action. Some years ago I worked at a large downtown shrine church that my order runs in Boston. My principal ministry was with the neglected street people who flocked to that Franciscan center. From time to time I was asked to share my thoughts about this ministry at "brown bag lunch" talks which that church sponsored. On one occasion I proposed for my subject, "Eucharist as Subversion." On the morning of the talk an older Franciscan confrere came and told me they had gotten my title wrong. "Didn't you mean 'Eucharist

as submersion,' Joe?" he asked. "No," I said, "they got it right—
subversion."

What I meant and what I said that day was that as partici-
pants, not just spectators, at Eucharist we truly become actors in
Christ's saving death and resurrection. That means when we
share in the Lord's Supper we are a continuation or an extension
of what his death and resurrection accomplished: overthrowing,
undermining, *subverting* everything that stands in the way of full
human liberation—all the violence, the poverty, the environmental destruction that keep people enslaved in any way. The Lord's
Supper, then, is a consolation *and* a challenge. It is *not* a tranquil-
izer. It's subversive.

The ritual of the Eucharist points to this revolutionary dimension in place after place. Right after the words of institution at
each Mass, the whole gathering affirms that "Christ has died;
Christ is risen; Christ will come again." A moment later we say
"Amen" to the One "through whom, with whom and in whom
all glory and honor are yours almighty God, forever and ever."
Saying these prayers clearly makes us part of the subversive action of the crucifixion. When we say them we are making them
our own. Or, as it is sometimes said, "with our 'Amen' we 'sign
our names' to Jesus' action."

At the end of each eucharistic celebration we receive once
again the charge to "go in peace to love and serve the Lord and
one another." That love and service, which Jesus modeled in his
life, clearly include justice and equity for all. That's subversive.
That's our "dangerous memory." Because the powers that maintain the status quo in this world, the ones at the service of the
empire, always see any movement to overcome injustice, inequal-
ity, institutionalized violence, and impoverishment as a serious
threat to their privileged positions—a threat that has to be eliminated. To paraphrase a chilling gospel text that referred to Jesus,
the empire always considers it better for the subversives to die
than for the whole imperial apparatus to perish.

This means that there is a "price tag" on Eucharist. We get no
free passes once we participate in it. No "cheap grace" is possible
here. The Eucharist demands that everyone who dares to celebrate it do what it signifies—overcome, combat, *subvert* every
form of sin and evil. I believe that the way those poor Bolivian

women broke their fast showed this same understanding of Eucharist. As rural, functionally illiterate indigenous folk they probably would not have articulated this conviction just this way, but the fact that they ended their remarkable and ultimately successful struggle against an unjust and abusive government by participating in Jesus' Paschal Mystery tells us that they understood Eucharist as a subversive activity.

So many other examples of the worldly and subversive aspects of Eucharist come to mind. Just to recall one. Some years ago torture survivor Sister Dianna Ortiz held a silent vigil of protest in front of the White House in Washington. She had been pressing our government for information regarding the American who walked into the hellish torture center in Guatemala City where she was being held, stopped her attackers, and took Dianna out of the place. Who was that man, she wanted to know. What gave him so much power in a Guatemalan torture center? And what of the others left behind, whose screams, Dianna said, she could still hear? For months and months our government stonewalled, refusing to give her any information about her case. Finally, in desperation, Sister Dianna went to the White House and sat outside that center of power for several weeks in silent vigil, hoping to force the Clinton administration to explain America's connection to the dreadful place where she had been brutalized.

Part of her vigil spanned Holy Week and Easter, so on Resurrection morning a large number of us gathered with Dianna and celebrated the Eucharist. The theme we chose was "who will roll away the stone" (Mk 16:3), an obvious Easter reference to the stony silence coming from that symbol of the empire in front of us. It was a bittersweet event. We knew that Dianna and the rest of us were continuing Jesus' own struggle against evil in this world, and we had faith that in the end resurrection would have the last word. But we also knew that more than likely the stone sealing off the facts about Dianna and her tormentors would not be rolled away. The stakes were too high for our government to reveal how an American had such authority in a Guatemalan torture center. In that regard we were all too correct. To this day she has not found out anything about U.S. complicity in her torture. Nevertheless, our sharing of this "dangerous memory," the Eucharist, in front of a temple of power that day, felt absolutely right. It was one more lived example of Jesus' subversive dying and rising.

There is an interesting footnote to that Mass. When it was over, a reporter from a national magazine covering Dianna's vigil drew me aside and asked, "What's going on in the Catholic community these days? I notice that all of you are pretty typical, middle-class, churchgoing people, and yet here you are on an Easter Sunday morning doing a very radical thing—bringing your [subversive] ritual to the very door of the White House." He had, of course, gotten it just right—Eucharist is a public action, outwardly oriented and a challenge to the powers and principalities of this world. If only every one of us Catholic-Christians could keep this in mind as a vibrant part of our spirituality each time we gather with the community around the table for the revolutionary act that is the Lord's Supper! We would change the face of the earth.

St. Paul's Challenge

This take on Eucharist as subversive is not new, much less something I made up. Right from the beginning the followers of Jesus celebrated the Lord's Supper in memory of one who took on the unjust power structures of his time, let himself be crushed by them, and in the end triumphed over them. The best example of this original, dynamic understanding of Eucharist comes out of St. Paul's first letter to the Corinthians, where he explains how he came to know this great gift: "For I received from the Lord what I also handed on to you, that the Lord Jesus on the night when he was betrayed took a loaf of bread, and when he had given thanks, he broke it and said, 'This is my body that is for you. Do this in remembrance of me.' In the same way he took the cup also, after supper, saying, 'This cup is the new covenant in my blood. Do this, as often as you drink it, in remembrance of me'. For as often as you eat this bread and drink the cup, you proclaim the Lord's death until he comes" (1 Cor 11:23–26).

We know these words—we've heard them every year on Holy Thursday when we commemorate in a special way the gift of the Lord's Supper, and again on the Feast of the Body of Christ,

Corpus Christi. The problem is that the part we hear has no frame of reference, no mention of the context in which they were written. It's as if Paul put these thoughts on paper in a vacuum—and that is a stunning oversight on the part of people who line up scripture readings for each day of the year. Because in this section of his letter to that early church at Corinth, Paul is really angry with those early Christians because of the way they were doing their eucharistic celebrations. Just before the verses quoted above, Paul writes: "Now in the following instructions I do not commend you, because when you come together it is not for the better but for the worse. For to begin with, when you come together as a church, I hear that there are divisions among you; and to some extent I believe it. . . . When you come together, it is not really to eat the Lord's supper. For when the time comes to eat, each of you goes ahead with your own supper, and one goes hungry and another becomes drunk. What! Do you not have homes to eat and drink in? Or do you show contempt for the church of God and *humiliate those who have nothing?* What should I say to you? Should I commend you? In this matter I do not commend you!" (1 Cor 11:17–22, emphasis added).

St. Paul obviously draws a direct line from the celebration of the Lord's Supper to communal, social justice. He tells the community that it is dangerous, to the point of blasphemy, to celebrate the one without at least trying to take care of the other. Paul finishes up his rebuke to the Corinthians with these chilling words: "Whoever, therefore, eats the bread or drinks the cup of the Lord in an unworthy manner will be answerable for the body and blood of the Lord. . . . For all who eat and drink without discerning the body, eat and drink judgment against themselves" (1 Cor 11:27, 29). What I hear in this message is that it would be better not to attempt a eucharistic celebration at all if they are going to continue "humiliating those who have nothing."

For our faith community today in the heart of the empire and as members of a transnational church, it's a very short step from Paul's critique of that ancient community at Corinth to our own realities. Eating and drinking the body of Christ without concern about all the hungers of the human family and our country's responsibility for them is eating and drinking judgment against ourselves. To put it another way, remembering that the Eucharist is celebrated in places like Iraq, North Korea, Sudan, Rwanda, and the decaying inner cities of the United States puts a claim on us as we gather to "do this in memory of me." We first-world Catholic-Christians simply cannot refuse to be aware of all the deprivations that our sisters and brothers in the household of faith and beyond suffer today across the planet. The Eucharist is outwardly oriented and subversive, demanding that all who participate in it be outwardly oriented and subversive as well. This has to be part of a real spirituality.

The remarkable story of Colombian priest Camilo Torres points in the same direction. As I came to know about him from people who had contact with Camilo during the 1950s and 1960s, I learned that he grew up as part of the privileged class of his country. But when he began to work in pastoral ministry after priestly ordination, he saw firsthand the social extremes that exist in Colombia. Soon he began to wonder about the Eucharist in that socio-political context. Camilo gradually took to heart the warning that Jesus laid out in his Sermon on the Mount: "If you bring your gift to the altar and there recall that your brother has anything against you, leave your gift at the altar, go first to be reconciled . . . and then come and offer your gift" (Mt 5:23–34).

Finally, the young priest decided that he could not offer the gifts at the altar until he did something about the terrible injustices that existed (and continue to exist) in his country. More specifically, he felt obliged to reconcile with brothers and sisters in the poorer classes who had something against him because of his privilege. Torres left priestly ministry and joined one of the guerrilla movements in Colombia, hoping to reform his country's injustices toward the poor that way. A short time later he was killed.

This story has always given me pause. On the one hand, if we in our churches here in the empire took literally the words of Jesus about leaving our gifts at the altar until we reconciled with alienated brothers and sisters, we'd never be in a position to present the bread and the wine for the Lord's Supper. As individuals and as a nation we occupy places of overwhelming privilege in the world, and numberless people have much against us. All we have to think of in this regard are the thousands of innocent Iraqi people killed or maimed by our aggression against their country, or the millions in the world who live on US$1 a day or less. On the other hand, we come to offer our gifts and celebrate Eucharist thanks only to God's mercy, not because we have reconciled with everyone who has something against us. Camilo Torres's example reminds us, again, of the "price tag" that the Lord's Supper carries. In a graphic and tragic way I believe that this priest echoed St. Paul's strict warning to the early Christian communities not to eat and drink the body and blood of the Lord without discernment—and in our case, with a great sense of repentance.

Another story makes the same point in a slightly different way. The great American missioner Father Vincent Donovan, C.S.Sp., spoke and wrote brilliantly about his life among the Masai people in East Africa as that indigenous community came to accept the Catholic-Christian faith. One of the remarkable lessons he received from these new Christians had to do with the way they celebrated the Eucharist.

On the day when the priest was coming for Mass these farming people gave over practically the entire day to the Liturgy of the Word and the Liturgy of the Eucharist. Early in the morning, before going out into the fields, they would pray as a community. Later, they would come back together for the scriptural readings and reflection, then return to their work. In the afternoon, when the priest arrived, the community would gather once again to break the bread and share the cup.

One day, Donovan relates, the elders of the community met him on his arrival and said: "Today we will not bless the bread and the wine." (Notice that right from the start they used *we* in speaking about the Lord's Supper.) The reason they gave for not blessing the bread and the wine that day was because "the grass has stopped." Grass is an all-important reality for the Masai, their life force. If a drought occurs and the grasslands dry up and wither, the entire community runs the risk of losing the crops and herds of cattle that are vital for survival. So when the Masai became Christians and began to celebrate the Lord's Supper, they chose a fistful of fresh grass, passed from one person to another, and from one family to the next, as their sign of peace, the sign that all was well with the community. On this particular day, however, part of the community had either not passed the grass or a part had not accepted it. "The grass has stopped"; that is, there is serious division, and thus no Eucharist is possible. They didn't try to paper over the problem with some quick-fix reconciliation and go ahead with the liturgy anyway. They knew they couldn't. The community was split, and, as Donovan reported, it was some time before the problem among them was resolved and they felt they could again "bless the bread and the wine."

These new Catholic-Christians knew instinctively that the Lord's Supper has very practical consequences; it carries a "price tag." They knew that Eucharist questions our behavior and is subversive of all that stands in the way of freedom, unity, justice, peace, and love.

Intentional Eucharistic Communities

Seedlings of eucharistic spirituality around today are the intentional eucharistic communities. The ones I know function outside parish and diocesan structures but are explicitly Catholic. They are led by lay people. As one of the priests who serve the sacramental needs of several of these communities, I've found that they fill a need for people who otherwise might not have a worship home.

Intentional eucharistic communities in this country remind me of the base Christian communities of Latin America, where people gathered for all sorts of purposes. One community in the Washington DC area came together around social justice issues. Another came into being in reaction to some heavy-handed policies of their parish priest.

A third community I have known for over thirty years first emerged at the suggestion of a visionary pastor who saw that a particular group of people in the parish had the creativity to plan liturgies which would nourish them. Now, after three decades, that experiment has succeeded beyond anything that priest could have imagined. While no longer connected to the parish, the original group has grown to a hundred or so families, with second and third generations continuing the high-quality eucharistic celebrations that the first pastor had envisioned.

What has most impressed me about these intentional eucharistic communities is the great care they take in the preparation and execution of their Sunday celebrations. Only those priests who commit to working collaboratively with the lay leaders and who make their own the themes decided on by the planning groups are invited to celebrate with them. In one of the communities, celebrants and lay planners gather each week for a shared reflection on the readings for the following Sunday. Together they determine how the liturgy will unfold—the thrust of the homily, appropriate music and communal prayers, an accompanying meditation. Eventually every member of the community, and all the priests who serve them, take a turn in planning the Masses. It's a deepening and stretching process and really helpful in developing a eucharistic spirituality.

Without exception, the intentional eucharistic communities take on problems and issues of the day. It couldn't be otherwise. It's impossible to get that involved in preparing good liturgies without being affected by the outward and subversive thrust of Eucharist, as we've been reflecting on in this chapter. These communities show enormous interest in and commitment to all sorts of social needs. One I know has sponsored and supported several immigrant families in its neighborhood; another regularly serves at a soup kitchen and night shelter; a third consistently holds up the pressing political and/or social questions of the day for prayer and action. Announcements at the Sunday celebrations are filled with updates and requests regarding the various issues and activities in which members are engaged. I always find myself deeply impressed during the announcement time at the end of the Mass. I think of these moments as the "nerve center" of the community.

Intentional eucharistic communities are probably not for everyone, but they do have the potential for deepening the spirituality of people who find them as a kind of oasis in the often top-heavy and impersonal institutional church in the United States. They are at least worth a look for people who are not satisfied with their worshiping community. I've found that the lay leadership of the intentional eucharistic communities takes responsibility for maintaining the Catholic identity of the group, for inviting quality presiders, and for insisting on reverent liturgical celebrations. We priests who serve them are constantly challenged to meet these expectations, particularly in the area of relevant homilies and in coming to understand that gender inclusivity with regard to language, dialogue, and participation are high priorities in their celebrations. When preparation and execution come together well in these unique communities, the result is a model of church in the world that reminds me of Jesus' words at the Last Supper, "If I washed your feet—I who am Teacher and Lord—then you must wash each other's feet" (Jn 13:14)—a real servant model.

One downside to these intentional eucharistic communities comes from the institutional church itself, which in my experience has yet to appreciate the value of welcoming them into the life of the larger body. If they could become official, non-territorial parishes in a given diocese, I believe that their vitality, creativity, and insights would renew the face of the church in the United States—and God knows we need that kind of renewal for a church that is generally silent here in the empire these days. As it is, pathetically few of them have been acknowledged, much less accepted by bishops in U.S. dioceses, a situation that shortchanges both the dioceses and the communities themselves. Quite simply, the official church is failing to take advantage of quality people and quality experiences by ignoring these new graces of the Holy Spirit. And that's a tragic loss.

Another problem area for intentional eucharistic communities is a direct result of this lack of official recognition. I'm afraid that not finding an official niche in parish and diocesan structures can compromise and weaken the Catholic identity of these communities over time. The danger is that neglect on the part of the institutional church could make them sort of elitist splinter groups that lack the diversity, stiff challenges, and bracing correctives that life in the larger church community, despite all its shortcomings, inevitably brings.

As an example of what I mean here, a major part of my ministry these days is centered in a multicultural diocesan parish. Founded by African Americans in the 1940s when they were not welcome in the white parishes of northern Virginia, the parishioners have welcomed a succession of Euro-Americans over the past six decades, and more recently Latin Americans. It's a remarkable and generally successful story. However, the challenges connected with taking care of the needs of this diverse church community—making sure that all of the backgrounds, cultures, and traditions present there are honored—keep all of us alert and humble. This parish still sees itself as a work in progress. The intentional eucharistic communities I know do not usually experience those sorts of challenges. They tend to attract like-minded people who form a fairly homogenous group.

Nevertheless, even with these problem areas, intentional eucharistic communities represent a gift to the church and, I hope, a wave of the future. Lay directed, communal in design and practice, using consensus in their decision-making processes, outwardly oriented and centered on word and sacrament, they are a haven for many people who crave better quality in their public liturgical prayer, who are fed up with an often stodgy parish life, or who have run up against the all-too-common experience of clerical and institutional rigidity. They stand as a sign of hope for the church in the United States and as a source of solid eucharistic spirituality, and they well may become the desperately needed prophetic voice of this church of ours that is situated in the midst of the empire.

Presiders

The reflection on intentional eucharistic communities and how careful they are in choosing celebrants brings me to say something about us who have the great privilege and the enormous responsibility of carrying out the eucharistic rituals.[1] The way the priest celebrates the Eucharist is crucial to its effect on people and significant in fostering a eucharistic spirituality. One time a very good and holy older priest commented to me that he understood why some people, especially young people, find so little inspiration at Mass that they rarely, if ever, attend. "There are presiders," he said, " who make the Eucharist unbelievable." This came from a kindly man not usually given to criticism, and his words stuck with me.

There was a time when this defining role of the priest wasn't so obvious. When Latin was the language at Mass, when the priest "did his thing" up there at the altar and there were hardly any clues as to what was going on, people felt that the ritual it-self did the job no matter how well or poorly the priest carried it out. While that sort of mechanistic understanding of the way our sacramental system works was probably never totally ac-cepted in our faith community, today people surely expect to get a lot more out of our celebrations. All that was said earlier in this chapter about actively engaging in the Lord's Supper means that the way it is celebrated by the priest, the lectors, the ministers of communion, and so forth makes an enormous difference.

Some years ago a bishop wrote a fine letter to the priests of his diocese about presiding at Eucharist. He made the point that this ritual is "theater"; it's the presentation of something that is dra-matic, that ought to be inspiring, and that is profoundly impor-tant for priests and laity. For many years a teacher of drama at the Catholic University of America held seminars for presiders, going over with them "the mechanics" of leading a eucharistic celebration. He was very entertaining, as he imitated, for ex-ample, the difference between a presider who shuffles into the sanctuary with his head down and no expression on his face and one who walks in alertly, obviously interested in who is present and convinced of what is about to happen. The same teacher demonstrated the difference between greeting the congregation with a quick and slurred "thelordbewithyou" and an inviting, heartfelt "the Lord is with you." He got lots of laughs and nods of the head as his listeners recognized the varying styles of pre-siding, including some of their own foibles. Those imitations of the indolence and seeming indifference of some presiders re-minded me of an instructor in rhetoric who once told me that the first rule for public speakers is physical alertness (he called it animal vitality): "your body language should show that you be-lieve you are about to say and do something important." The eucharistic celebration really is theater.

People who know about liturgy say that the presider walks a tightrope at Mass. He has to "present" the ritual, avoiding over-dramatizing the action and making himself the center of atten-tion while also avoiding the tendency to "underwhelm" the com-munity with a passive approach to the rite. The presider is neither a showman nor a robot. He "stands behind" the eucha-ristic action and lets it speak for itself, but at the same time he needs to let the congregation know that he believes and reverences what is taking place.

The same is true for the other ministers of the liturgy. Those with musical gifts greatly help the assembly to "pray twice," as music is often called. It's always a pleasure and a religious experience to be part of eucharistic celebrations at which instrumentals and songs complement and highlight the scripture readings for that particular day. But the music shouldn't take over the celebration or, worse, become a performance that competes for attention with the re-presentation of the Lord's Supper. Lectors who read the biblical texts for the community often bring biblical passages alive after preparing and proclaiming God's word with conviction. Their reading is an art. And many times I've found myself greatly edified during the distribution of holy communion when a lay eucharistic minister next to me says a word or makes a gesture that expresses his or her deep faith in what both of us are doing—sharing the presence of Christ.

At the end of the day I believe that for all who minister around the altar the crucial question comes down to believing, really believing, in what we are doing at the altar, coupled with a humble attitude. To put faith in Jesus' words, "Do this in memory of me," and to know that the eucharistic action is Christ's, not the priest's or the other ministers'—spells the difference between good and poor celebrations, between people's eucharistic spirituality being fed or starved, and often between the Eucharist being an adrenalin or a narcotic.

To carry that kind of responsibility, I believe that presiders, in particular, need all the help we can get from the members of the communities we serve. And I think that people should not hesitate to tell us how we come across in trying to lead the community in this central act of our faith. Some years ago a priest whom I knew well found himself in a serious vocational crisis. His attitude at the altar reflected what the poor man was going through—he was listless and self-absorbed. One evening, after a particularly unimpressive celebration, a leading lay man in the parish took the priest aside and strongly urged him to get help for whatever problems were getting in the way of appropriate and life-giving eucharistic celebrations. Of course that was a terribly hard message for the priest to hear, especially in the midst of his own difficult circumstances. However, it was offered in a loving way and with obvious concern for the priest himself, as well as concern for the centrality of Eucharist in the life of that faith community. Fortunately, the priest did seek help and eventually came to some peace. It would be good if more people did that kind of a favor for priests—and perhaps other ministers—who fail to make the Eucharist a life-giving experience because their actions show a lack of preparation and interest or because of the way they move through the ritual. At the same time, lectors who prepare the readings, and homilists who deliver thoughtful and challenging messages, and the musicians, priests, and other eucharistic ministers who try to present the Lord's Supper in a way that nourishes and challenges ought to get regular affirmation from the community. In the parish where I serve it is not uncommon to hear applause from the congregation after a particularly relevant homily or at the end of a joyous and relevant Mass.

Conclusion

Everything I've written in this chapter comes out of something I had to think about seriously while still in Latin America—that life and liturgy need to make an impact on each other. It's a simple concept but all too often proves difficult in practice, at least from what I've observed and what people tell me—"There's no connection between our lives and the Mass." For me, the years in Bolivia and Peru, where I saw so much poverty and oppression, forced me to make the connection between the causes of human suffering and Jesus' dying and rising. One of my stories from those years will help, I believe, bring this chapter on Eucharist to a close.

Some friends of mine in Lima once took an automobile trip through the Peruvian Andes. About midday on one leg of their journey they stopped for lunch in a remote pueblo and went into a little restaurant. As they sat down to eat, an extremely poor Indian woman came in and asked them to let her have any scraps of food they might leave behind. My friends called the boy who was serving the table and told him to bring a plate of food for the woman and charge it to their bill. She gratefully took the food and went outside into the warming sunshine to sit and enjoy this unexpected windfall. As my friends watched, another person in the same impoverished condition came along and sat down beside the first woman. They said that they fully expected her to tell the second woman to go inside and beg for her own meal. But she didn't do that. Instead, she looked around the ground and found a piece of old cardboard lying there. She brushed the dust off of it and pushed half of her meal onto the cardboard for the other woman to eat.

That story always makes me think about Eucharist and the many facets of this incredible gift. How can we not connect the bread of life, recognizing Jesus in the breaking of the bread, with all the efforts to feed the poor and all the efforts the poor make to feed themselves—like the two women in this story. These connections strike me as the very center of Christian spirituality, and not to make them leaves eucharistic celebrations in the dry limbo where too many of them end up. Making these connections helps us remember that spirituality has everything to do with active engagement in the here and now, in the real moment where each of us lives our life. I think this story also puts Jesus' statement that we shall always have the poor with us in a different light. While doing our best to eliminate poverty, we know that, like those two Andean Indian women, the poor often are our teachers, helping us to deepen our life in God through engagement with God's world.

Postscript

My experience in Latin America and afterward has convinced me that the ideal and challenge of a preferential option for the poor can be the unifying principle that holds together the several dimensions of Catholic-Christian spirituality. The conscious choice to see everything through the eyes and experience of the impoverished masses in our world strikes me as another of those new graces given by the Spirit for our times.

The idea of a gospel bias in favor of the poor, of course, is rooted in both the New Testament and the Hebrew scriptures. Chapter 2 of this book makes that point clearly, I hope. Its modern articulation comes from a remark made by Pope John XXIII in 1959: "The church wants to be the church of all people, but in a special way the church of the poor." A few years later the *Pastoral Constitution on the Church in the Modern World* from the Second Vatican Council began with the words, already quoted in Chapter 5: "The joys and hopes, the fears and anxieties of the men of this time, *especially those who are poor or in any way afflicted,* these too are the joys and hopes, the fears and anxieties of the followers of Christ" (emphasis added).

It was the Latin American church which gave us the right words to use in describing this gospel imperative. Several times in this book we've mentioned the Medellín conference held during August 1968, where representatives of every national bishops' conference in Central and South America met and called the entire household of faith—bishops, laity, religious, and clergy—to stand with the poor. From then on the official pastoral approach of the Catholic Church in that part of the world was based on the preferential option for the poor.

The liberation theologians took up the task of unpacking this ideal, as they based their new way of doing theology on the lived experience of the oppressed majorities in Latin America.

Through that special lens the theologians looked at God's word from a unique perspective—that of the poor—and saw that oppressed, dispossessed, and marginalized people hold what they called a privileged place in God's eyes and in salvation history. This was what the bishops were driving at when they called for the whole Latin American church to make a preferential option for the poor. It was a move to the side of the poor, in behalf of the poor—and in behalf of those who are not poor as well. We people of privilege need to get near to the poor for our own sakes, because that's where we will most surely meet God.

The preferential option for the poor has become part of the church's vocabulary, far beyond Latin America. For example, most Catholic religious congregations by now have called their members to make this bias toward the poor a conscious option in their lives; many have taken steps to implement it in their collective decisions, for example, by assigning significant numbers of their personnel to ministries with the poor, as well as putting finances, buildings, and land at their disposal. The bishops of the United States in their 1986 pastoral letter *Economic Justice for All* weighed in on this gospel call with these words: "As followers of Christ, we are challenged to make a fundamental 'option for the poor'—to speak for the voiceless, to defend the defenseless, to assess life styles, policies and social institutions in terms of their impact on the poor" (no. 16).

Of course it was inevitable that such highly charged words—preferential option for the poor—and the radical idea they express would meet with opposition and rejection. How could it be otherwise, given the unsettling challenge such a choice represents for people of privilege—not to mention what it means for the empire? To quote Jon Sobrino, a preeminent Catholic theologian who looks at us with special clarity of vision: "The manifest destiny of the empire is 'the good life.' No need to ask about the price that the poor of this world have paid and must still pay for that life."[1]

One complaint about this option, for example, holds that God does not have any preferences but loves every one of us equally. Others say that the option for the poor excludes everyone who is not poor, and that's against the gospel. These are half-truths that we could argue about semantically for a long time. However,

I've found that the quickest and best way to cut through these objections is to return to Jesus' words about the final judgment on all our lives expressed in Matthew's Gospel. After telling us what the basis for that judgment will be—what we did or did not do for the hungry, the thirsty, the naked, the lonely, the stranger, and the imprisoned—the Lord makes a giant leap further and says, "I assure you as often as you did—or did not—do it for one of these, the least of my brethren, you did—or did not—do it for me" (Mt 25:31–46). Jesus himself opted for the poor in an incredible way—by actually identifying with them.

Still, because the preferential option for the poor continues to be controversial, too often in Catholic-Christian circles otherwise nice, moral people think that maybe we shouldn't grapple with what it calls us to do. Controversy is not a nice state of affairs. In our U.S. society differences often get swept under the rug. Tolerance and politeness have high priority and that terribly bland attitude of "whatever" describes many people's reactions to opposing views. But, when you think about it, controversy was the most obvious hallmark of Jesus' life and ministry. He was always in conflict with the power structure of his country. He took sides and demanded that his followers do so too. Options are what gospel living is all about. He said it clearly—"You cannot give yourself to God and money" (Mt 6:24), and in a hundred other ways.

In the final analysis, in spite of or perhaps because of its controversial nature, I have come to believe that the preferential option for the poor is one of those Catholic-Christian insights that is instinctive. We don't need great argumentation or theological explanation to "get it." The call to opt for the poor stands there as a self-evident and stark gospel choice, and we have to deal with it. As Jon Sobrino says: "Taking an option for the poor means taking an option for reality. It means deciding for real participation in reality. So the option for the poor is not something extraordinary, let alone esoteric. It also should not be thought of as the ultimate way of being Christian and human, but rather as a first, fundamental step."[2]

It may be that we've gotten too accustomed to hearing about the option for the poor. Indeed, some say that perhaps a lot of the impact of this call has dissipated over the years and it only gets lip service nowadays. That would be a pity, because especially for those of us who live in this culture at this time in history, an option for those who are left out is essential if we are to rescue the soul of our people and our society. I believe that deep down our Christian hearts tell us that at this time and in this place the preferential option for the poor must ultimately inform and influence everything we are about as individuals and as a faith community. It gives us a unifying principle for our spirituality. How we incorporate it into our lives as people of faith living in the heart of the empire will be the final test of that spirituality.

In the end, after all is said and done, the choice for us is stark: serve the reign of God or serve the empire. No middle ground is possible.

"Blessed are you poor, the reign of God is yours" (Lk 6:20).

"How blessed are the poor in spirit, the reign of God is theirs" (Mt 5:3).

Notes

Preface

1. Jon Sobrino, S.J., *Where Is God?* (Maryknoll, NY: Orbis Books, 2004), viii.
2. *Washington Post Book World*, October 29, 2006.
3. Vincent Miller, *Consuming Religion: Christian Faith and Practice in a Consumer Culture* (New York: Continuum, 2004).

2 Political Reading of the Scriptures

1. Gustavo Gutiérrez, *A Theology of Liberation* (Maryknoll, NY: Orbis Books, 1973), 47.
2. For a contemporary story of how the prophetic tradition in the Hebrew scriptures entered a debate between people of faith and representatives of the International Monetary Fund, see page 121 herein.
3. Ched Myers has developed in detail and with real scholarship the Jubilee theme and its direct applications to current history. See especially *Binding the Strong Man, Who Will Roll Away the Stone?* and *Say to This Mountain*, all published by Orbis Books.
4. World Synod of Catholic Bishops, *Justice in the World* (1971), no. 6.

3 Prayer and Contemplation

1. Marie Dennis, Joseph Nangle, O.F.M., Cynthia Moe-Lobeta, and Stuart Taylor, *St. Francis and the Foolishness of God* (Maryknoll, NY: Orbis Books, 1993).
2. Thomas Merton, *Conjectures of a Guilty Bystander* (New York: Image Books, 1968), 156.
3. Dorothy Day, *Commonweal* 67 (December 1957): 330–32.
4. Oscar Romero, homily given February 17, 1980, in *The Violence of Love*, comp. and trans. James R. Brockman, S.J. (Maryknoll, NY: Orbis Books, 2004), 205.

5. Martin Luther King, Jr., "I Have a Dream," address delivered at the March on Washington for Jobs and Freedom, August 28, 1963, Washington DC.

6. Mahatma Gandhi, *Harijan* (English weekly founded by Gandhi) (December 11, 1938), 328.

5 Obedience

1. For the story of that parish, see Joseph Nangle, O.F.M., *Birth of a Church* (Maryknoll, NY: Orbis Books, 2004).

6 Poverty and Chastity

1. Gustavo Gutiérrez, *A Theology of Liberation* (Maryknoll, NY: Orbis Books, 1973), 289.

2. Francis of Assisi, "How St. Francis Taught Brother Leo That Perfect Joy Is Only in the Cross," *The Little Flowers of St. Francis* (the "Fioretti"), trans. Raphael Brown (New York: Doubleday/Image Books, 1958), 58, no. 8.

3. Jon Sobrino, S.J., *Christology at the Crossroads* (Maryknoll, NY: Orbis Books, 1978), 214.

4. A. W. Richard Sipes, *Sex, Priests, and Power—Anatomy of a Crisis* (New York: Brunner/Mazel, 1995), 67–68.

7 The Church and the New Creation

1. Joseph Nangle, O.F.M., *Birth of a Church* (Maryknoll, NY: Orbis Books, 2004).

2. I'm using *reign of God, kingdom of God,* and *New Creation* interchangeably. However, I like the phrase *New Creation* because it carries a much more dynamic and forward-moving sense, one that I think captures best what Jesus was talking about in his preaching.

3. This paragraph is all about the church as institution, and I include in my criticism not only our current group of bishops but priests and deacons who Sunday after Sunday have access to pulpits in this land and, with few exceptions, fail to educate and challenge their people to act on these enormously important New Creation problem areas.

8 Ecology

1. Leonardo Boff, *Ecology and Liberation: A New Paradigm* (Maryknoll, NY: Orbis Books, 1995), 7.

2. The Franciscan theological tradition makes an extraordinary claim about Christ and creation. The fascination that Francis had with the incarnation led the great thinkers in the order to assert that even if sin had not appeared in the world, God's Word would still have become human.

3. Jonathan Harr, *A Civil Action* (New York: Vintage Books, 1996). Touchstone Pictures made the book into a movie in 1998; the movie was nominated for two Oscars.

9 Eucharist

1. This section has to do with priestly ministry, particularly our role as presiders at the Eucharist. As I write it, I am all-too-painfully aware that in our tradition this role is open only to a small fraction of the Catholic population—celibate males and a few married men who have come over from the Episcopalian Church. As an ordained priest in the Catholic Church I can only acknowledge this huge discrepancy and work toward the day when stirrings of a vocation to priestly ministry among married people and particularly among women will be taken seriously by my church.

Postscript

1. Jon Sobrino, S.J., *Where Is God?* (Maryknoll, NY: Orbis Books, 2004), xii.

2. Ibid., 69.

Index

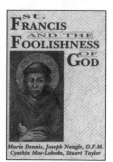